MONARCH
OF THE
GREEN

YOUNG TOM MORRIS
PIONEER OF
MODERN GOLF

STEPHEN PROCTOR

First published in 2019 by

ARENA SPORT
An imprint of Birlinn Limited
West Newington House
10 Newington Road
Edinburgh
EH9 1QS

www.arenasportbooks.co.uk

ISBN: 978-1-909715-75-2
eBook ISBN: 978-1-78885-166-4

British Library Cataloguing-in-Publication Data
A catalogue record for this book is available on request from the British Library.

Designed and typeset by Polaris Publishing, Edinburgh

Printed by TJ International Ltd, Padstow

CONTENTS

One

HERO'S WELCOME

———————— • ◉ ⬤ ◉ • ————————

As the ten o'clock train chugged into St Andrews, Young Tom Morris's admirers hustled out to Station Road beside the golf links to welcome their champion home. It was Saturday night, 17 September 1870. By then everyone had heard the news. Young Tom had done it. For the third year in succession he'd won the Champion's Belt, the trophy every one of Scotland's leading golfers dreamed of fastening around his waist. Now it was Tommy's to keep.

Since Thursday, when news of his feat had filtered into town, the Scottish flag had flown over his father's golf shop heralding the victory. But it wasn't the win alone that brought Tommy's faithful out that night. It was the way he had played. Tommy had annihilated all records for the Open Championship, coming in with a score so low it would stand for the ages.

He was 19 years old.

Even at that age, Young Tom Morris was the defining player of his era. He stood five feet eight inches tall, with reddish-brown hair like his father's and a wisp of a moustache. He was thin and wiry but capable of surprising strength, more likely than most to snap his wooden shaft in half with a ferocious swing. He dressed like a dandy, favouring tailored suits, silk ties and pocket watches, and he played the game with a reckless abandon that dazzled those who saw him compete.

'I shall never forget – and no one can – his dash and style,' recalled the Reverend William Weir Tulloch, his father's first biographer. 'His grand swipes, the Glengarry bonnet flying off his head every time he took a full drive.'

Young Tom was accompanied on the train from Prestwick, birthplace of the Open Championship, by his father, Old Tom, his best friend and competitor David Strath, and fellow golfer Bob Kirk. The four of them had made it a clean sweep for St Andrews men, with Davie and Bob tied for second and Old Tom in fourth. Not a single player from Musselburgh, St Andrews' chief rival in golf, had finished in the top rank, making victory all the sweeter.

Tommy had barely stepped off the train when his worshippers, much to the champion's delight, swept him up onto their shoulders and, with deafening cheers that roused the sleepy town, carried him all the way up the links to Mr Leslie's Golf Inn. Inside they were greeted by a crowd of well-wishers that included every star in the golfing firmament of St Andrews.

The first to speak was James Glover Denham, a close friend of the Morris family. Denham had been injured in a railway accident and couldn't play golf any more. But he was a devoted fan of the game known for the copious statistics he kept on leading players of the day. He proposed a toast to Tommy's health. Young Tom, he said, had performed a feat that in all probability would never be repeated. He had brought St Andrews the highest honour a golfer could confer on the town and raised the profile of Scotland's national game.

Then Tommy himself raised a glass. He thanked the crowd for its warm demonstration of affection and told them something no one in that room could have known, except perhaps Old Tom and Davie. Two years ago, when he was just 17, Tommy had made up his mind that it was his destiny to own the Belt. He would be the golfer who ended the decade-long quest for that red-leather trophy, with its gleaming silver buckle. He would be the one who earned the right to wear the Belt for all time by winning three consecutive Open Championships. Tonight, Tommy said, he relished the satisfaction of a dream realised.

His father spoke next. Old Tom had won the Open in consecutive years himself, losing narrowly in his attempt to claim the Belt with a third victory. It was his pleasure, he told the crowd, to see that coveted trophy worn by his greatest rival on the links, his own son.

Henry Farnie, who covered the Open for the *Fifeshire Journal*, must have sensed a passing of the torch from Old Tom and the great players of his day to Scotland's new Champion Golfer. Old Tom was nearly 50 now. With his thick grey beard and ever-present pipe in hand, he was well on his way to becoming the most revered figure in the game. Farnie raised his glass to offer a toast of his own. To Old Tom Morris, he said.

The revelry went on into the night, as everyone in Mr Leslie's savoured the opportunity to witness history – and, perhaps, took a turn trying on the Belt. They knew that golf had never witnessed a feat to match what Young Tom had accomplished two days ago on the links of Prestwick.

But they could not have known that by winning the Belt he was forging a new future for the royal and ancient game. Ever after golf would be driven by the feats of superstars like Tommy, coming along once in a generation, lifting the game onto their shoulders and carrying it to new heights.

Emboldened by his victories, Tommy set in motion changes that in decades to come would elevate the men who earned their living at golf, from disreputable caddies not welcome in any gentlemen's clubhouse to men of stature with wealth of their own.

Tommy's emergence would prove to be the pivotal moment in golf's evolution from a Scottish pastime to a spectator sport, ushering in a period of phenomenal growth that saw the game spread to England, America and around the globe.

So lasting was Tommy's impact that a generation later, during the 1896 Open at Muirfield, his memory was invoked by those who had come to see the game's next prodigy, Englishman Harry Vardon, who would win the first of his record six Open Championships that year.

The question, inevitably, was who was the greater golfer. William Doleman, a baker from Glasgow, spoke from the perspective of a man who had competed in every one of Tommy's Opens. His assessment was unequivocal.

'I tell you, sir,' he said in response to a question from a friend. 'There isn't a man, English or Scotch, in all this field that impresses me with the same sense of power, or golfing genius – call it what you like – as Tommy did the instant he addressed the ball.'

Sadly, those who toasted Tommy into the night at Mr Leslie's also could not have known that all of his glorious achievements, before and after the Belt, would be eclipsed by personal tragedy. Or that it would be James Denham, the very man who raised the first glass to the champion, who made certain the young golfer's fame was etched in stone forever at the most sacred place in St Andrews, the cathedral's burying ground.

Two

PRESTWICK

························ •●●●●• ························

In a sombre ceremony on 19 April 1850, surrounded by ancient stone walls and ruins, Tom and Agnes Bayne Morris's first-born son was laid to rest in the cathedral cemetery at St Andrews. The boy they called Wee Tom, after his father, was a month away from his fourth birthday.

Parents in the Victorian age knew their children might die young, as so many babies did, but the chances diminished with each year that passed. Wee Tom was not a baby any more. His death was more than any parent should have to bear. The inscription on his tombstone, still visible in that old churchyard, captures his parents' anguish and their faith: 'In the silent tomb we leave him, till the resurrection morn, when his saviour will receive him and restore his lovely form.'

Tom and Agnes, whom friends and family knew as Nancy, had been happily married and increasingly prosperous for six years before that crushing blow. They would be together another two and a half decades, years in which the Morris family would be destined to experience more than its fair share of both unbridled joy and unremitting sorrow. The dark cloud that descended over the couple when Wee Tom died was lifted almost exactly a year to the day later. On 20 April 1851, Tom and Nancy welcomed into the world another son. In the custom of the era, he too was named Tom Morris Junior.

Young Tom arrived at a time of upheaval in the Morris household. His parents were about to move to Prestwick, on Scotland's west coast. Tom had been hired to lay out a proper golf course there and work as keeper of the green. That was a dream job, but it meant leaving the only home the couple had ever known, that old, grey town by the sea. Tom and Nancy could not have had any inkling of it then, but moving from St Andrews to Prestwick would give their newborn son the starring role to play in a drama about to unfold in the game that provided the family's livelihood.

Tom and Nancy had grown up at a time when weaving linen by hand was a booming business in St Andrews. Tom was born in 1821, Nancy three years earlier. Both of their parents were hand-loom weavers, as were nearly all the families living on North Street, a thoroughfare that cuts through the heart of the town from the links to the cathedral churchyard. Weavers lived in two-room stone cottages, with the front room devoted to the loom and the back to living space and beds. If the family made fine linen, running the loom was a tough job reserved for the man of the house. Weaving coarse linen, however, as the Morrises did, demanded less physical strength and could be handled by wives and daughters. In either case, it was a cramped, difficult, hand-to-mouth existence.

In the early 1800s, St Andrews was a town of 4,000 souls that had become decidedly down-at-heel. Before the Scottish Reformation, it had flourished as the spiritual capital of a Catholic nation. Pilgrims flocked to its famed cathedral to receive blessings at the shrine of St Andrew, Scotland's patron saint. The two centuries since had seen steady decline. By the time Tom and Nancy were born, the cathedral had long since gone to ruin with livestock roaming freely on the town's narrow, filthy streets.

Not surprisingly, given that it was home to the most famous links in the land, golf was inextricably intertwined with life in St Andrews. The town was considered then, as it is now, the capital of the Scottish game. If it had any rival for that title it was Musselburgh, then home to The Honourable Company of Edinburgh Golfers, one of the oldest clubs in the kingdom. But the Musselburgh links paled by comparison to that of St Andrews, which in every age has been considered the ultimate test of a golfer's skill.

'The links of St Andrews – of The Royal and Ancient Golf Club of the East Neuk of Fife – hold premier place as indubitably as Lord's Ground in the kingdom of cricket,' the great British amateur and golf writer Horace G. Hutchinson wrote years later, summing up a sentiment that had prevailed since the first player struck a ball. 'All the great mass of golfing history and tradition – principally, perhaps, the latter – clusters lovingly within sight of the grey tower of the old university town, and to most the very name of St Andrews calls to mind not a saint, nor a town, nor a castle, nor a university, but a beautiful stretch of green links with a little burn, which traps golf balls, and bunkers artfully planted to try the golfer's soul.'

Weavers like Tom's father, John, had always been among the regulars on the St Andrews Links. Linen merchants paid them by the yard, not the hour, so they were free to set their own schedule. That usually included playing golf and working as a caddie to help pay for it. By the time Tom and Nancy came of age, the Industrial Revolution was nearing its apex, and it was clear there would be no future in hand-loom weaving. Nancy became a domestic servant in the home of a prominent St

Andrews couple. Tom was apprenticed to Allan Robertson, the town's famous golf ball maker.

Every golfer who grew up in the 19th century – and Young Tom would have been no exception – was steeped in the legend of Allan Robertson. A small, feisty, jovial man, Allan sported bushy mutton chops that were fashionable in the 1800s and often wore a bright red jacket that was a popular uniform for golfers in the game's early years. He was considered the greatest player of his generation – Scotland's 'King of Clubs' – and was the first to hole the course at St Andrews in fewer than 80 strokes. Everyone in town recognised Allan as the unofficial custodian of the links and undisputed authority on anything having to do with golf. So beloved was Allan that when he died in September 1859, an admirer from The Royal and Ancient Golf Club, A. Gordon Sutherland, exclaimed, 'They may toll the bells and shut up their shops in St Andrews for their greatest is gone!'

Becoming Allan's apprentice opened a new world to Tom – a world of big-money golf matches that brought him wealth, fame and social advantages that would give Young Tom a head start in the game and in life. 'Allan had a great deal to do with the making of me,' Tom acknowledged at the dawn of the 20th century, when he had emerged as golf's elder statesman. By the time he and Nancy's second son arrived – they were married in 1844 – Tom had become a genuine golf celebrity. He had earned a reputation throughout Scotland as Allan's toughest rival and had become a favoured partner of leading members of The Royal and Ancient.

Four years after his marriage, in 1848, Tom walked away from his apprenticeship and opened his own shop, which new research shows was located at 15 The Links. It was a perfect time to be starting a business. A few years earlier, in 1832, town provost Major Hugh Lyon Playfair had launched improvements that would bring new life to St Andrews and its famed links. The area would emerge as a thriving Victorian town built around the University of St Andrews, the prestigious new secondary school Madras College and the revered golf course. Tom made both clubs and balls at his new shop and, along with the money he won at golf, earned a far more comfortable living than most Scots born into a family of craftsmen.

Tom and Nancy's future seemed set, until he received the job offer in Prestwick. It came from Colonel James Ogilvy Fairlie, a pillar of Scottish society, a gifted sportsman and Tom's frequent golf partner at St Andrews. Fairlie and Tom were made for one another. Both were men of dogged determination and unflappable temperament and Fairlie also ranked with the best amateur players of his day. In 1862 he won the medal at all three of his golf clubs. He and Tom made a great pairing in a foursome or any other venture. Tom admired Fairlie so much that he would name a son after him. Still, moving all that way from St Andrews must have been a daunting prospect for Tom and Nancy. They may have had any number of reasons, beyond Tom's respect for Fairlie, for accepting the post at Prestwick. Perhaps Tom wanted to step out of the long shadow Allan cast in St Andrews. Perhaps he and Nancy simply wanted a change of scenery after the death of their first-born son.

Whatever the reason, the Morrises set out for a new life on the west coast of Scotland when Young Tom was just three months old. It's hard to imagine now what an arduous journey that would have been, loaded down as they were with their belongings and Tom's club- and ball-making tools. The 100-mile trip would have taken at least eight hours, and would have involved a bumpy ride in a cart from St Andrews to Leuchars Station, three train changes, luggage and all, and one trip aboard a ferry. Poor Nancy had to endure the entire ordeal with a babe in arms.

In July of 1851, when the Morris family arrived, Prestwick was a town of 2,000 people situated along the road that leads to

Ayr, the Royal Burgh and county seat of Ayrshire. Half the size of St Andrews, Prestwick was surrounded by farms that supplied Glasgow, the region's largest city, with vegetables and milk. They also gave the town its name. Prestwick is derived from Old English words that translate as 'priest's farm'. The centre of town was marked by the Mercat Cross, a symbol of prosperity in burghs granted the right to host markets or fairs. It stood where the three main roads in Prestwick converged, flanked by offices and shops. The most prominent among them were the Burgh Hall and the Red Lion Inn, home to Tom's new employer, Prestwick Golf Club. Years later, as the town grew, the Cross was moved to a quieter intersection.

The cottage the Morrises occupied, which came to be known as Golf House, stood directly across the street from the Red Lion. The layout would have been familiar to Tom and Nancy, as it was nearly identical to the stone cottage they had left behind in St Andrews. Tom's shop occupied the front room, with the family's living and sleeping quarters in the back. Rent was £6 a year, deducted from Tom's generous salary of just under £50, five times what local farmers were making.

The Morrises' neighbours across the street, Red Lion proprietors William and Elizabeth Hunter, would become their closest friends in Prestwick. Their eldest son James would be among Tommy's childhood companions. Years later, James would marry Tommy's sister and make the Morris family a fortune in the timber business. Both the Red Lion and Golf House still stand in Prestwick, although the town's oldest pub is a faded jewel and Tom and Nancy's cottage is unrecognisable, having been converted into a cafe.

During their years in Prestwick, Tom and Nancy would have three more children. Elizabeth arrived in 1852, James Ogilvy Fairlie Morris, or Jof, in 1856, and John in 1859. Poor John, to whom Young Tom would be especially close, was born with a hip deformity that could be corrected easily today. It left him unable to walk all his life and confined him to a trolley his father made for him.

Young Tom and his siblings grew up in a difficult period in Victorian Britain. The potato blights of 1845 and 1846 made food scarce everywhere and sent millions fleeing to America in search of a better life. Many children survived on nothing more than bread, porridge, oatcakes and beer. The situation wasn't as bad in lowland Scotland, where Tommy's family lived, as it was in much of the rest of the nation. Families there often had gardens and could supplement their diets with vegetables. Those who were better off, like the Morrises, could afford some eggs, sausages and meat, but even then the lion's share would be reserved for the man of the house, whose work put food on the table.

Unless their family was extraordinarily wealthy, children who grew up in that age knew hunger as a constant companion. Even as late as the 1890s, when the food supply was greatly improved, the author of the Winnie-the-Pooh books recalled constant cravings during his boarding school days at Westminster College. 'I lay awake every night thinking about food,' wrote A.A. Milne. 'I fell asleep and dreamt about food. In all my years at Westminster, I never ceased to be hungry.'

If the lack of food wasn't trying enough, the work involved in day-to-day living was absolutely exhausting. In this age of technology, it is easy to forget that every task – from cooking to cleaning to personal grooming – was vastly more difficult and time-consuming in that era. Both parents and children worked tirelessly simply to keep the household going. These stark realities tend to be overshadowed by the quest for progress and remarkable discoveries that have come to define the reign of Queen Victoria.

Not much is known about Young Tom's earliest days in Prestwick. But there can't be any doubt that whatever free time he had was spent on the links his father laid out in Ayrshire. If Old Tom's own childhood is any measure, his son would have been taking his first swings with a cut-down club as soon as he could walk. In an interview decades later, Tom recounted his own start in the game as a boy in St Andrews. 'I began, then, to play golf down here, I am quite sure, as soon as ever I was able to handle or swing a club,' he said. 'Indeed, I must say that I don't remember when I didn't play, and I have been doing not much else ever since.'

Young Tom must have spent hours chasing shots around the sandy dells of Prestwick. By the time he made his first public appearance at the age of 12, he had earned a reputation as a prodigy. His childhood golf partners were James Hunter and Johnny Allan, son of a local stonemason. They were tough competitors. As young men, both won the Eglinton Medal presented by The Prestwick Mechanics' Golf Club, an organisation for working-class players. Later both competed in the Open Championship. Johnny went on to devote his life to golf, working at The West of England Club in North Devon, better known as Westward Ho!

Precocious as he was in golf, Tommy's parents clearly wanted their eldest son to be prepared for a life beyond the club- and ball-making shop. He hadn't been attending the Burgh School at Prestwick long before he and James were enrolled at the prestigious Ayr Academy, which has educated such famous sporting Scots as rugby captain Ian McLaughlan and Olympic gold medal curler Margaret Morton. Founded in 1796 and still ranked with the nation's finest schools, the Academy was an expensive investment for the Morris family. It cost more than a shilling a week, compared to a penny at the public school. That amounts to nearly 5 per cent of Tom's annual salary. The Academy was also three miles from home. Travelling that distance every day would have been no easy matter.

At the Academy, Tommy traded the clothes his mother favoured – in the fashion of the day, Nancy dressed her son in sailor's togs – for a jacket and tie. He sat beside the sons of wealthy merchants and landed gentlemen, learning to be at ease in their company. He studied an array of subjects far wider than what was available at the Burgh School, including astronomy and Latin, science and philosophy. Tommy wasn't as gifted a student as James, but the experience made an indelible impression on him. Never again would he accept the notion that he was inferior to gentlemen golfers, a second-class citizen not welcome in their clubhouses. That would become clear years later when Tommy emerged as a driving force in elevating the status of men who earned their keep from Scotland's national pastime.

The ideas Tommy absorbed at the Academy were reinforced by sweeping economic, social and political changes brought on by the Industrial Revolution. Tommy came of age at the height of that transformative era when men first became enchanted by machines and the possibilities they presented. It was an age of factories replacing artisans, of railroads replacing horse-drawn carriages, of a newly born working class overwhelming the ranks of farmers, craftsmen and seafarers.

The same year his parents moved to Prestwick, thousands flocked to London to ogle the latest inventions – the cotton gin and the telegraph, the microscope and the barometer, the daguerreotype and the voting machine. Queen Victoria's husband, Prince Albert, had assembled them at the Great Exhibition of 1851, the first in a series of World's Fairs that became popular in the 19th century. Three years earlier, Europe and Latin America had been swept by political revolutions, ultimately unsuccessful, that were sparked largely by demands from the downtrodden for relief from the harsh realities of industrial life, the grim working and living conditions described so vividly in the popular novels of the day by Charles Dickens.

The quest for improvement had come to golf five years before Tommy's birth. In 1846 a ball made from gutta-percha, the sap of trees that grow on the Malaysian Peninsula, began circulating around St Andrews, Edinburgh and Musselburgh. At the time, golf was being played with the feather ball; before that players had used wooden ones. The feather ball got that name because it was made by stuffing hen, duck or goose feathers into a leather casing and sewing it together. The result was a hard, somewhat oblong ball, whose influence on the early years of golf is impossible to overstate.

Making featheries created a class of craftsmen – such as Allan and Tom – who, along with caddies and greenkeepers, became the first men to make their living from golf. More importantly, the ball was so expensive that few men who weren't wealthy could afford to play the game, at least not with proper equipment. An experienced workman might make four featheries a day. A single ball cost more than a golf club and players were lucky if one survived two rounds, given that featheries often burst open in wet weather. Gutta-percha balls were ten times less expensive to make and many more people could afford them. They were also virtually indestructible. A ball damaged during a round could simply be heated up and remoulded.

Men like Allan, whose family had been making featheries for generations, saw the new ball as a threat to their livelihood. He forbade Tom and his other employees from playing with the gutty, as it was known, and went so far as to pay boys to fetch them from the links so he could burn them in his shop. Once, in a comical scene, Allan asked his caddie to tee up a gutty so he could show his fellow golfers how inferior a ball it was. He took a mighty swipe, purposely topping the ball, and remarked in feigned disgust, 'Ach, it winna flee eva.' To which his caddie promptly replied, 'Flee, damn ye, nae ball cud flee when it's tappit.'

It was a tiff over the gutty that led Tom to quit his apprenticeship. The break came one afternoon in 1848, when

Tom was playing a round at St Andrews with Fairlie's brother-in-law James Campbell, a handsome and popular member of The Royal and Ancient Golf Club. By the time they reached the turn for home, Tom had lost all of his featheries. It was easy to do in those days, when the course was extremely narrow and lined with thick gorse bushes. Campbell gave Tom a gutty to use, and he immediately started playing better than he had been while spraying all of his featheries into oblivion. As Tom and Campbell were finishing their round, Allan was starting out on his. Inevitably, they crossed paths on the crowded links.

'It so happened,' Tom recalled years later, 'that we met Allan Robertson coming out, and someone told him that I was playing a very good game with one of the new gutta balls, and I could see fine from the expression on his face that he did not like it at all and, when we met afterwards in his shop, we had some high words about the matter, and there and then we parted company, I leaving his employment.'

It was a losing battle. Gutties were so cheap that within a few years the feathery was dying out. By the time Tommy was born, it was virtually extinct and even Allan had taken to making gutties.

The gutty did not revolutionise the game because it flew farther than the feathery. The great leap forward in distance would not come until the 20th century, with the invention of a rubber-cored ball known as the Haskell. The longest drives ever recorded with a gutty and a feathery were of comparable length. A typical drive with either ball flew 200 yards or less. Distance aside, however, the gutty was a far superior golf ball. Unlike the feathery, it could withstand the pounding of iron clubs, which would radically change how golf was played. It also putted vastly better than its predecessor, which wasn't truly round. That made the toughest part of the game easier for every player.

Nothing that had happened until then – and nothing that has happened since – changed the game more dramatically than the coming of the gutty. Golf would no longer be the private preserve of gentlemen, as it had been to a large extent in the feathery era. The arrival of the gutty tilted the scales. It made golf affordable for everyone, and in the decades to come, thousands of new players from all walks of life would be drawn to the game. Wealthy gentlemen would continue to hold the positions of power and influence in golf, which even now is viewed as an elitist sport. But as Scotland's national pastime grew exponentially, so too did the ranks of men who earned their living by tending greens, making clubs and balls, or carrying clubs, along with playing golf for money on the side. Laughable as it may have seemed at the time, these were the men who would one day gain the upper hand in the royal and ancient game.

One of the first clubs to sense what this tilting of the scales might mean for the future of golf was not a member of the old guard, The Royal and Ancient in St Andrews or The Honourable Company in Musselburgh, but the newly formed club in Prestwick. It is a curious side note that Allan's fruitless effort to quash the gutta, the ball that started the revolution, paved the way for Tom Morris – and especially his gifted young son – to be living at Prestwick during that extraordinary moment of change.

Three

THRUST AND PARRY

———————— • ● ◉ ● • ————————

Golf had been played for over 400 years before Young Tom was born and almost never the way it is done today: every man for himself and the lowest score wins. Tommy grew up in golf's 'age of match play'. During his childhood, the most popular way to play the game was foursomes, a format many modern golfers experience only in club competitions or international contests such as the Ryder Cup.

In foursomes, two golfers team up and play alternate shots from tee to green until their ball is holed. They might play against another pair of golfers or against a field of two-man teams. Foursomes became golf's game of choice because it had everything players of the age wanted. It depended upon camaraderie, it was devilishly difficult and it was wildly unpredictable. Even picking a partner involved subtle strategy. Should two men with similar games pair up? Or should a long driver choose a steady putter? Would two partners inspire one another or drag each other down? How would one man react if his partner hit a shot that left him playing the team's next one from desperate trouble? The complexities were endless – and sublime.

If a foursome couldn't be had, golfers preferred to face off man to man. In both cases, matches were decided by who won the most holes, not who came in with the lowest score. Stroke play, the dominant game today, was usually a last resort. The universal popularity of match play, foursomes in particular, makes a powerful statement about the way players viewed the game when Tommy was a boy. Golfers of that age weren't fixated on their score the way players are today. They were perfectly content to play a game in which they hit only half the shots. Grinding out a low score was considered a dreary business, vastly inferior to the thrill of hand-to-hand combat. 'The match was the thing, and the keenly contested foursome rather than the exclusive single,' wrote golf historian H.S.C. Everard.

It was this unquenchable thirst for thrust and parry and the drama it generated that first demonstrated the Scottish game's potential to become a popular spectator sport. In the early years of the 19th century, while Tommy's father was Allan's apprentice, gentlemen gamblers took to staging big-money matches between artisan golfers, the crack players who emerged from the ranks of caddies and ball makers. A betting man from St Andrews, for instance, would put up £100 and issue a challenge to any man willing to match the stake and find a player to take on his favourite golfer. These challenge matches, sometimes singles, sometimes foursomes, captured the imagination of fans and drew increasingly fervent crowds. Old Tom and Allan both made their reputations playing in them.

Playing foursomes was also every gentleman's favourite way to spend an afternoon at his club. A typical day at Prestwick Golf Club, or any other, would involve two foursome matches, one played in the morning, the other after lunch. Having arranged a match, members would consult their resident authority on golf to determine if any strokes had to be given to make for a fair fight. Old Tom played that role at Prestwick, as Allan did at St Andrews. Their ability to size up members – the caddie's natural instinct for knowing his man's strengths and weaknesses – was a highly prized skill. Handicapping systems like those that golfers use today would not develop until the turn of the century.

Club members never played without a caddie, usually the same man for every round, and were easily spotted on the links. Most of the caddies wore a uniform, usually a blue or red blazer with a handsome tie, fashionable waistcoat and ornate buttons made especially for their club. When their matches ended, gentlemen would spend the rest of the evening at a sumptuous dinner, swapping stories about their heroic deeds before heading home with a belly full of mutton and claret. In their earliest years, club members dined in rooms at inns like the Red Lion. Before long they would build lavish wood-panelled clubhouses that became their private inner sanctums.

Golf clubs may have been private, but the links weren't. Joiners, masons and seafarers were out on the course too, as they had been since the time of Tommy's grandparents and great-grandparents. Beyond the obvious disparities in class and comforts, a working man's golf life wasn't all that different from that of his wealthier counterpart. Playing the game was among the rare occasions in which men of vastly different classes had something in common. Working men competed in foursomes or singles just as gentlemen did. They wore jackets and ties too, although theirs weren't as stylish and they couldn't be bothered with uniforms. Every golfer, however shabby his clothes might look, needed multiple layers for comfort in Scotland's brisk, blustery weather. Working men also looked forward to a bit of post-round fellowship, although it's a safe bet that their toasts over a pint at the public house were more ribald than those raised at stately dinners for gentlemen.

The biggest difference in the golfing lives of working men was that most of them couldn't play nearly as often as gentlemen did. Only caddies and ball makers, whose lives revolved around the game, could play as regularly. Club men were often landed gentry who didn't need a job; they could take to the links three or four times a week. Working men had gruelling schedules. Their leisure time amounted to a few precious hours to spend playing the game they loved. Once the gutty came along, making it possible to afford a proper ball, artisans began forming their own clubs and staging their own competitions, including one to ring in the new year. They were, however, outnumbered by gentlemen golfers. When Old Tom helped found The Prestwick Mechanics' Club in 1851, it had 28 members. The course's fledgling club for gentlemen had nearly twice that number, and St Andrews ten times as many.

Among both lords and labourers, golf was an exclusively male bastion in Young Tom's day. It wasn't as if women had never played. There had been a few recorded instances of ladies on the links. In 1738 a couple of married women played at Bruntsfield Links, with their husbands as caddies, and in 1811 Musselburgh staged a competition for fishwives. But those were rarities. The truth is that Victorians were horrified by the image of a woman swinging away in a fashion that must inevitably reveal her ankle and perhaps her leg. The prevailing view was that proper women's golf did not extend beyond putting. Even then it wasn't until 1867, when Tommy was a teenager, that a Ladies' Putting Club, with its separate putting course, was formed at St Andrews, the first in the world.

When the press paid any attention to golf, it focused solely on gentlemen. No one reading their local newspaper would have known that working men played the game, unless some unlucky craftsman was caught trying to sneak in a round on the Sabbath. The spotlight shone most brightly on gentlemen golfers during the spring and autumn meetings of major clubs, when members gathered to take care of business and compete for time-honoured prizes. Since 1744, when the City of Edinburgh bought a silver club to be played for annually on the Links of Leith, kings and noblemen had been supplying cups and medals that gentlemen battled for every spring and autumn. Local newspapers provided fawning coverage, something closer to society news than sports reporting, noting the names of the winners and those of prominent nobles in attendance, especially at the sparkling party that concluded the week's festivities.

These medal competitions were among those last-resort occasions when golfers abandoned match play and tried to make their way around the links in the lowest possible score. Clubs had long ago discovered that with nearly every member on hand, the only sensible way to manage these events was to award the silver club or gold medal to the player who took the fewest strokes. Even smaller mechanics' clubs for working men had to compete at stroke play in their tournaments. Golfers submitted grudgingly to playing with a card and pencil, but they admired men who could post low scores. When Allan came in with the first 79 on the Old Course in 1858, it caused a sensation. Still, every golfer's passion was for a friendly match. Players could not get back to foursomes quickly enough. Chances are no one saw the need to count strokes on the biggest days of the year as a portent of changes that would unfold over the decades to come.

Whatever the format, golf in Young Tom's day was all about gambling, proof that while golf balls and clubs may be radically different in the modern age, the soul of the game has changed not one whit over hundreds of years. Since the 1760s, and perhaps earlier, leading gentlemen's clubs had kept bet books recording every wager between members, a handy document to have if a dispute arose in the clubhouse. Most bets were on foursomes, whose volatility made them ideal for wagering. Joiners and seafarers may not have had bet books to provide proof to future historians, but there can't be any doubt that they also laid down a bob or two before heading out on the links.

Typically, gentlemen golfers staked a crown on the match and a shilling on each hole. Those were substantial wagers for a man playing several times a week. A hundred of those crowns could keep a working-class family in house and home for a year. But it is likely that victories and defeats evened out over time and no man won or lost too much. Bets on matches weren't the only action available in the clubhouse. There were also wagers akin to the proposition bets offered today at gambling casinos. Members would bet one another, not only on who would win the club's gold medal, but also on how low a score the winner might post.

If two gentlemen wanted an especially spicy match with a heftier stake – and they often did – each would take as his foursome partner one of the best players on the grounds, a caddie or club and ball maker who made his living at the game. These men played for tips from the gentlemen who recruited them. If their side won the match, they might get as much as 10 per cent of the stake. Their share would be far more paltry if they lost. These caddies and ball makers were the first men to be known as professional golfers. But the word didn't mean then what it does today. They weren't called professionals because they were the best players in the game. The word branded them as members of an inferior class. Gentlemen did not have to scrape for a living the way these working-class men did.

Betting on their own foursomes was never enough to satisfy the thirst that wealthy gentlemen had for action. Many major clubs also took to staging high-profile singles and foursome matches between professionals, with the stakes put up by well-heeled members backing their favourite players. These events proved such a lively entertainment for the lords and ladies on hand – not to mention another chance to lay down a bet – that it became a point of pride for clubs to lure the best golfers to their spring and autumn meetings. Newspapers sniped at clubs that didn't put up enough money to attract Scotland's finest.

These matches also provided sorely needed income for professionals, whose patrons, as always, rewarded them based on how the match turned out. Because so many men, like Tom's mentor Colonel Fairlie, belonged to more than one club, spring and autumn meetings were scheduled to avoid conflicts. That helped them evolve into the first competitive circuit for professionals. Twice a year, professionals travelled to St Andrews, Musselburgh, Prestwick, North Berwick and beyond in the hope of fattening their purse. That could never have happened had it not been for the rapid expansion of affordable British railways during the 19th century. Even men of modest means, who once found it all but impossible to venture far from the city in which they were born, now had the entire country at their disposal.

Two years before Young Tom was born, interest in battles between professionals was ratcheted up by the most famous high-stakes foursome in the early history of golf. Tommy and every other player of that era would have grown up hearing tales of The Great Foursome of 1849, the defining event of golf's age of match play. It was the first competition between professionals to be covered extensively by local newspapers, which seldom ventured beyond club medal days and battles involving gentlemen. The match would be talked and written about well into the next century.

The foursome pitted Tom and Allan against identical twins Willie and Jamie Dunn, who were reigning champions of Musselburgh. The two towns were natural rivals – St Andrews the genteel haven of the upper class, Musselburgh the grimy working man's town. Gamblers who arranged the match set the stakes at £400, an extraordinarily extravagant sum at that time. Tom would have had to work ten years to earn that much money, and even his cut of the winnings would have represented a healthy portion of his annual salary. He and Allan may have gone their separate ways in the shop, but they weren't about to break up their partnership on the links, where they could rake in the pounds.

The Great Foursome would be played over three courses – 36 holes each at St Andrews and Musselburgh, followed by the deciding rounds at a neutral course, North Berwick. Marathon battles were the norm in the age of match play and considered the true test of a champion. As always, the match at each of the three links would be won by the team that took the most holes. But in those early years, when a foursome was played over multiple courses, there was a twist. The match would go to the team that won on two of the three courses, not the one that won the most holes over the length of the competition. The Great Foursome of 1849 would prove that was no way to determine a winner.

From start to finish, interest in the match was at fever pitch, with throngs of spectators turning out to follow the players around the links. By the third and deciding contest – each team won at its home course – passions were running so high that a special train had to be arranged from Edinburgh to North Berwick to ferry all the fans clamouring to attend the finale.

Professional golf in 1849 was more like prizefighting than the sedate game we know today, with fans hushed for every shot and television announcers speaking only in whispers. At The Great Foursome, as was the case at all golf matches in those days, fans cheered and heckled loudly and scrambled all over the links to see how their team's shot turned out. They weren't above crowding close to an opponent while he was trying to swing or kicking his ball into trouble if their side needed help. It would be two decades before anyone came up with the idea of containing fans behind a gallery rope. Betting on every match was heavy, with gamblers roaming the fairways and shouting out new odds for wagers as the fortunes of the contest ebbed and flowed.

On the final day of the competition at North Berwick, the enormous crowd was overrun by rowdy Dunn fans from neighbouring Musselburgh and matters nearly got out of hand. 'I never saw a match where such vehement party spirit was displayed,' wrote golf historian H. Thomas Peter. 'So great was the keenness and anxiety to see whose ball had the best lie, that no sooner were the shots played than off the whole crowd ran, helter-skelter; and as one or the other lay best, so demonstrations were made by each party. Sir David Baird was umpire, and a splendid one he made. He was very tall, and so commanded a good view of the field, but it took all of his firmness to keep tolerable order.'

The Dunns would have won easily if the score had been kept by the number of holes won – as it would be forever after this match – instead of by which team won on two of the three courses. With his powerful, syrupy swing, Willie Dunn was one of the longest drivers of his day, capable of hitting the ball 250 yards in an age when a shot of 200 yards was considered a mighty swipe. He and Jamie won at Musselburgh by the laughable score of 13 holes up with 12 to play, while Tom and Allan squeaked by at St Andrews with a win on the final hole. Allan was off his game throughout the match, causing fans to joke, 'That wee body in the red jacket canna play gouf!'

The Dunns were four holes up as the match wound down at North Berwick, and anyone interested in betting on Tom and Allan could get odds of 20/1. But one by one, thanks mostly to Tom's dogged perseverance, the Dunns let the holes slip away. At the 35th hole, the brothers had the cruel misfortune to hit their ball behind a huge stone on a cart track that ran alongside the links. Just as Tiger Woods would do in ages hence, the Dunns asked Baird to have the stone removed. The stately referee, a man described even by his friends as 'magnificent and pompous' said 'no'. He declared that the stone was part of the course and a fixture. One after another, Willie and Jamie flailed helplessly at the ball, eventually extricating it, but not before Tom and Allan took the lead and eventually the match. Boys idolise their fathers, and there can be no doubt that Young Tom swelled with pride whenever he heard again the story of how his father had saved the day for St Andrews.

It is no surprise, given the thrills provided by The Great Foursome, that every club in the land wanted to generate some of that same excitement at its spring and autumn meetings. It is, however, one of those unexpected turns of fate that these matches between professionals, intended merely as an amusement for club members and guests, evolved into golf's marquee events. It was the advent of a fundamental change in the game. By the beginning of the 20th century, the attention of the golf world would be increasingly focused, not on the gentlemen who had lorded over it for centuries, but on this growing class of professional players.

The reasons aren't hard to understand. Professionals had a much greater incentive to play well. It helped to put food on their table. They made shots and posted scores most gentlemen could only dream about. Their games were far more fun to watch, especially a slashing player like Young Tom. Amateurs who competed in the early Opens often turned in absurdly high scores. 'Think,' mused golf writer Bernard Darwin, 'of how many eights and tens and 12s must have been taken by Mr Moffat of persevering and illustrious memory who in the Open Championship of 1863 completed his three rounds of 12 holes apiece in 233 strokes.' Professional matches also raised the pulse by pitting players from rival towns against one another, as The Great Foursome had done, stoking the flames of partisanship at the heart of sports. Over the next two decades, high-stakes matches would attract breathless newspaper coverage and draw an army of new fans to golf.

Tommy was just three years old when the most audacious of these challenges was issued by a man who would emerge as the anti-hero of his childhood and his early years in the game, Willie Park. A cocky and gifted club and ball maker from Musselburgh, Willie was a rising star, a dozen years younger than Tom and nearly 20 younger than Allan. He had grown up as the son of a farmhand in a cottage a short iron away from the links, the best player in a family of great golfers. His brothers Mungo and David and his son Willie Jr. all ranked with the finest players of their age. Tall and strong, wearing his signature bow tie, Willie had a gaunt face and squared-off beard that made him look, especially in his later years, a bit like Abraham Lincoln. He was a deadly putter and a prodigious driver. Allan, who ducked every chance he had to play Willie man to man, freely admitted that, 'He frichtens us a' wi' his lang driving.'

In 1854, at the age of 21, Willie took the provocative step of publishing a challenge in *The Sporting Life* offering to put up his own money to play Allan, Tom, or his Musselburgh rival Willie Dunn in a singles match. When no one responded, Willie showed up at the autumn meeting of The Royal and Ancient Golf Club to confront his rivals face to face. Tom alone took up the gauntlet – and even then only after Willie had mercilessly thrashed his brother George. In a match for £50 a side, Willie handily defeated Tom on the St Andrews Links, going five holes up with four to play. It was the beginning of a rivalry that would dominate golf for decades.

The electricity generated by these challenge matches could not have come at a better time. In the early years of the 19th century, the game had been at a low ebb, struggling to survive even in historic centres like Edinburgh as financial troubles beset the landed gentry and the Industrial Revolution meant more work and less leisure time. Had it not been for the interest gentlemen gamblers had in staging high-stakes professional matches –

and the coming of a superstar like Young Tom to capture the imagination of reporters and fans – the future of golf would have been uncertain at best.

The size of the crowds that lined the fairways for these events planted a seed in the mind of Colonel Fairlie. It was the notion that golf needed to be bigger than a high-profile match or an annual competition between club members. He saw the future of the game as a contest that was national in scope. Not surprisingly, given his background and membership at both St Andrews and Prestwick, Fairlie's initial idea was to host a tournament for gentlemen golfers.

The Grand National Tournament featured two-man teams from prominent clubs playing foursomes in an elimination format. The trophy, interestingly, was a silver claret jug. Contested at St Andrews in July 1857, and repeated for the next two years, the event was such a hit that the *Fifeshire Journal* made this cogent observation: 'The excitement on the Links was greater than even on an October or May gathering of The Royal and Ancient. The supporters all along appeared to pay marked attention – crowding round the home hole on the return of the combatants.'

Flush with that success, and no doubt after communing with Tom, Fairlie refined his vision. He was too smart and forward-thinking a man not to have noticed that fans increasingly were turning out to see the seemingly miraculous feats professional players performed on the golf course. What Scotland needed, he decided, was a competition among them to crown an undisputed Champion Golfer. That was especially true at that moment, as the nation's acknowledged 'King of Clubs', Allan, had died the previous year. One of Fairlie's motives in starting a championship for professionals surely must have been giving Tom a chance to wear that crown.

In May 1860, a year before the Civil War broke out in America, Fairlie proposed that Prestwick launch a competition to identify Scotland's national champion. This would not be a match-play tournament, like its predecessor, but a stroke-play event, a distinction that would set the tone for the future. It would be conducted over 36 holes, or three rounds of the 12-hole course at Prestwick. Eleven of the most prominent clubs in Scotland would be invited to send their leading professionals to play, with the proviso that they be reputable caddies. Gentlemen golfers were still not ready to welcome just any ragtag band of professionals, however gifted.

Fairlie had hoped Scotland's other leading clubs would support this proposal as enthusiastically as they had the national competition for gentlemen. They were lukewarm to the idea, however, which is hardly surprising given that St Andrews had discontinued the Grand National Tournament because it diverted attention from the club's all-important autumn meeting.

Undaunted, Fairlie persuaded his fellow Prestwick members to purchase an ornate trophy for their new tournament. They chose a handsome belt made of red Moroccan leather. It was adorned with a large silver buckle embossed with golfing scenes and the coat of arms of the Burgh of Prestwick. Modern golfers might think, quite correctly, that it looks like something handed out at a prizefight. Inspiration for the choice came from the club's patron, the 14th Earl of Eglinton. He had previously given a gold belt to be competed for annually by boxers. Hand-crafted by James and Walter Marshall, Goldsmiths, Jewellers and Watchmakers of Edinburgh, the Challenge Belt cost the princely sum of £25.

In a letter written on 7 October 1860, Fairlie outlined the terms of the competition. 'A prize will be given by members of the club for professional players in the form of a highly ornamented Belt to be played for on Wednesday 17th, to be challenged for every year – until won by the same player three years in succession when it becomes his property.'

It was that final phrase that mattered. Any player who won the Belt could leave a £25 deposit with the secretary of Prestwick, keep the trophy for a year, and return it the following autumn. But the ultimate prize was to win the Belt outright, to establish a legacy as the Champion Golfer of this emerging age. Sadly, The Earl of Eglinton would not live to see that achievement. He died two years after the competition began.

Young Tom was nine years old, no doubt already demonstrating his gift for golf, when the first Open Championship was played. It is not much of a leap to imagine him, even then, dreaming of standing before an adoring crowd with the Belt wrapped around his waist.

The tournament that evolved into the major championship we know today grew in fits and starts. In Tommy's era it was not even known as the Open, no doubt because it didn't start out that way. Only professionals were allowed that first year. Gentlemen golfers were invited to play as amateurs the following autumn, making it a true open competition, but they were rarely a threat. There was no prize money at the first three Opens, but the competitors did get a very good lunch at the Red Lion. Prizes were added in 1863 – but still nothing for the champion – responding to a poor turnout the previous year. Beyond the chance to keep the Belt for a year, the winner earned nothing until 1864, when first prize was set at £6. Fields were small in those formative years, usually around 12 players, but so was the world of golf itself. The game was popular only in Scotland, and fewer than three dozen golf clubs existed.

The Open may have begun as a small event appended to the autumn meeting at Prestwick, but it represented a significant turning point in the game's history. From that moment on there would be regularly scheduled professional stroke-play tournaments, and their number would only increase. Every autumn the best players in the land made it a point to show up at Prestwick, paying their own travel expenses in the hope of earning money by working as a caddie, winning the Open, or pocketing a few pounds in matches. That speaks volumes about what professionals thought about this new championship.

Tom and Willie dominated the early Opens. Willie won the inaugural competition, much to the dismay of everyone at Prestwick. Tom had designed their golf course and put their club on the map. Naturally he was the heavy favourite. Tom came roaring back the next year to take the title that Fairlie had always hoped he would earn. He romped it again in 1862, winning by 13 strokes. That remained the largest margin of victory in a major championship until Tiger Woods won by 15 in the 2000 US Open at Pebble Beach. Tom seemed poised to claim the Belt as his own in 1863, but Willie was not about to let that happen. He evened the score at two Opens apiece.

While Young Tom would have been attending classes at Ayr Academy, it is impossible to believe that he, James and Johnny would not have found time to take in some of the action when Willie denied Prestwick's favourite son the Belt in that first championship and Old Tom carried the trophy home to Golf House the following year.

What was important about those early Opens, however, was not who won or lost. It was that they were the first golf competitions covered by newspapers outside Scotland. The Open had captured the imagination of London gamblers, whose interest in betting on the outcome brought out the English press. That would turn out to be pivotal to the growth of golf.

The stage was now set for the game to emerge from the age of match play into a new future, a transition that would gather unstoppable momentum during the decade-long quest to take possession of the Belt. The leader of this golf revolution would make his splashy debut in the spring of 1864, at a golf course in the 'Fair City' of Perth.

Four

MASTER MORRIS

W hen Tom Morris showed up at the Perth Open Tournament with his young son in tow, Willie Park was ready with a snarky question.

'For why have ye brought your laddie, Tom?' Willie needled.

'You'll see for why soon enough,' Tom shot back.

The year was 1864. Young Tom was not quite 13 years old, but his father apparently had decided the boy was ready for public competition. Father and son had taken the train 90 miles north-west to Perth, a port city on the River Tay that took its nickname from Scottish writer Sir Walter Scott's story *Fair Maid of Perth*.

Perth was the first town or city to catch the fever for professional tournaments that spread in the decades after the institution of the Open. The following year, St Andrews revived its professional tournament, a competition for caddies and ball makers that dated from the early 19th century. For reasons unknown, it had either not been conducted or not been mentioned in newspapers since Old Tom won it in 1842. It would be the only tournament other than the Open held on a regular schedule during those early years of professional golf. The St Andrews Professional Tournament was conducted at either the spring or autumn meeting of The Royal and Ancient and sometimes at both.

The Perth Open brought out all the leading professionals of the day: players like David Park, Andrew Strath, William Dow and local favourite Bob Andrews, in addition to Tom and Willie. The competition began on 12 April, but like other golf spectacles of that era it spanned several days and included a tournament for amateurs, a competition between clubs for working men, and the usual high-stakes singles and foursomes.

A steady sort, never one to overplay his hand, Old Tom planned to enter his son in the amateur event. But apparently Tommy's reputation had preceded him and Willie was one of the few wondering why Scotland's most famous golfer had brought his laddie. The men running the tournament barred Tommy from the amateur event. As the son of Scotland's leading professional, they ruled, he could not fairly be considered an amateur. They also decided Tommy wasn't old enough to take on the professionals, who had no interest in playing against a 12-year-old boy with a reputation.

It looked as if Tommy would not get to swing a club. But Joseph Smith, a member of one of the clubs sponsoring the tournament, saw an opportunity and seized it. He arranged a match between Tommy and a local player about the same age, William Greig. Stakes were set at £5. Greig had just won the Rector's Medal, a high-profile competition for Perth's young players. The win earned him a reputation as the region's rising star. Young William was made of tough stuff. He went on to be a scratch player at the Singapore and Shanghai clubs and a winner of the Straits Settlement Cup, the highest honour for golfers in South East Asia. Late in life he lost his right foot in an accident, but with the aid of a prosthesis he kept right on playing a steady game.

The match between Tommy and William took place over the North Inch of Perth, scene of one of the most momentous events in Scottish history, the Battle of the Clans. In 1396, an exasperated King Robert III sent two of his noblemen north to end the war between Clans Chattan and Kay, whose murderous raids on one another were threatening the stability of the realm. The nobles arranged to settle the dispute by having 30 men from each clan fight it out with swords on the North Inch. Clan Chattan's men killed every one of the warriors from Clan Kay, losing 19 of their own in the process.

Less than a century after that bloody confrontation, the only battles taking place on that hallowed ground were at golf. Perth was among the first places where the game was played, and the North Inch remains in business today as one of the world's oldest links. Tommy and William met there on 14 April, the kind of glorious spring day that justified the Fair City's nickname. Their match drew an enormous crowd, larger than the one that had followed the professional tournament two days earlier. 'It was very funny,' wrote local historian Peter Baxter, 'to see the boys followed by hundreds of deeply interested and anxious spectators.'

Hard-nosed as William was, he was no match for Young Tom. The impression Old Tom's laddie made in his debut is preserved in a newspaper clipping pasted into a scrapbook his father had begun keeping in 1850, using an old railway ledger. Unfortunately, the story reports only the outcome of the contest and never mentions the score.

'Perhaps the most interesting match of the day was between Master Morris, son of the redoubtable Tom, and Master William Greig, of, it seems, Perth juvenile golfing celebrity,' the newspaper reported. 'They are really wonderful players for their years, both of them. We had no idea that the young Perth could produce so proficient a golfer in Master Greig. He played with astonishing neatness and precision, but the honours of the day were in store for his competitor. Master Morris seems to have been both born and bred to golf. He has been cast in the very mould of a golfer, and plays with all the steadiness and certainty, in embryo, of his father.'

Baxter was moved to even greater accolades. 'The Perth Tournament of 1864,' he wrote, 'will ever be kept in remembrance as the first occasion on which the Admirable Crichton of golf, Young Tom Morris, engaged in public contest.' The reference to the Admirable Crichton is the highest compliment a native of Perth could bestow, as it referred to the region's most famous son, 16th-century genius James Crichton, known for his extraordinary gifts for language, arts, science and sports.

The golf world clearly believed it had witnessed the coming of a prodigy. Young Tom's match with Greig received more extensive coverage in the press than the professional tournament, which Old Tom won in a play-off against Willie by a commanding 14 strokes.

When the assembled professional players were gathered afterwards for a photograph to commemorate the event, Young Tom was invited to pose with them, a powerful indication of how the young star was viewed. A fresh-faced lad among his bewhiskered elders, dressed in his Sunday best, Tommy holds a club and rests his left arm on his father's shoulder. He stares intently into the camera, a confident young man who knows that he belongs with these professionals and might well have taken them down had he been given the chance. Tommy's first victory in a professional tournament was still three years away, but after Perth no one doubted it was coming.

Four months after Old Tom and his son returned to Prestwick – Young Tom no doubt arriving home as something of a celebrity – life would take another dramatic turn for the Morris family. Five years earlier, in the autumn of 1859, Tom's golf partner and long-time friend, Allan, had died of jaundice a fortnight before his 45th birthday. Allan had always been the unofficial custodian of the St Andrews Links, but he had his shop to tend to and various local golfers had been hired part-time to do the actual work of keeping the green. In the years after Allan's death, The Royal and Ancient Golf Club became unhappy with course conditions and decided it needed a full-time caretaker for what had long been considered a sacred golfing ground.

Naturally, the club turned to someone who had always been a respected figure in St Andrews, Old Tom. The R&A offered him a salary of £50 a year, a bit more than he was making in Prestwick. It came with the incentive of an annual budget that he could spend on improving the links, including hiring help when necessary. More importantly, the offer gave Tom and Nancy a chance to return to their beloved town by the sea, which was flourishing again thanks to its transformation by the late Major Playfair.

In August of 1864, Tom resigned from Prestwick Golf Club and prepared to move his family back to St Andrews, where he would emerge over the ensuing decades as the Grand Old Man of Golf. Prestwick sent him off in style, with a testimonial dinner that started in early afternoon at the club and went on into the night, at which Old Tom received the proverbial gold watch. The Morrises' best friends, William and Elizabeth Hunter, also held a special dinner for family and friends at the Red Lion Inn.

It was a period of change in Young Tom's life too. His friends James and Johnny left school to go to work, as most Scottish boys did when they reached their teens. Victorian families simply could not afford to allow more time for schooling. Their sons needed to begin earning money to help the family make ends meet. James was getting his start in the timber business at a cousin's timber yard. Johnny was working with his father as a stonemason, loathing every minute of it.

Given the sacrifices Tom and Nancy made to send Young Tom to Ayr Academy, it is reasonable to believe they had in mind for their son a career outside golf. No record exists of Young Tom being apprenticed in any field. That is telling because an apprenticeship involved a contract with the craftsman, who was paid to teach a young man his trade. But a few curious coincidences in 1865 suggest it is possible that after the family returned to St Andrews, Young Tom was sent to work in Glasgow.

Tommy is recorded as having competed professionally only twice in 1865. The first occasion was on New Year's Day at St Andrews, in a tournament conducted by the Operatives Club, an organisation for caddies and ball makers. The second was at the Open Championship that autumn. Curiously, he was entered there as 'Tom Morris, Jnr, from Glasgow'. The most compelling evidence that Tommy may have been working in Glasgow between those tournaments comes from historian Baxter. His book about golf in Perth includes a story that places Tommy in Glasgow at that time.

The story is about how Bennett Lang, the town of Perth's club and ball maker, came to learn his trade. In 1865, when Bennett finished his schooling, 'he was apprenticed to a firm of engineers in Glasgow,' Baxter writes. 'Here he met Young Tom Morris.' Baxter does not say that Tommy was working in Glasgow at the time. He says only that Bennett bumped into Tommy as the young star was playing golf. That leaves the question unanswered. Baxter goes on to say that Bennett and Tommy became friends. 'The intimacy with Young Tom Morris,' he writes, 'led to Lang going to St Andrews and learning golf club-making with Old Tom.'

If Young Tom had been sent to work in Glasgow, it was a short-lived career. By the spring of 1866 he was back in St Andrews, honing his emerging skills in that crucible of golf, playing against the local stars and those who came from neighbouring towns to test their mettle on the greatest links in the kingdom. Tommy clearly had room to improve. Even after his impressive showing at Perth, the 14-year-old had received strokes in the Operatives Club event on New Year's Day. That makes it clear what fellow professionals thought of Young Tom's game at the time. They didn't think he'd have a chance to win unless they spotted him a few strokes at the start.

His debut in the Open that September also ended ignominiously. He came in with scores of 60 and 57 on his first two trips around the demanding 12-hole course at Prestwick. Both were respectable rounds, especially given that he was only 14 years old. They left Tommy trailing his father by just a stroke. He was, however, nine strokes behind leader Willie Park and eight behind eventual winner Andrew Strath, Davie's elder brother. Andrew established a new Open scoring record that year with his three rounds in 162.

Perhaps it was the hill Tommy had left to climb. Perhaps, like any genius, he was disgusted by not living up to his own standards, as Bobby Jones was when he stormed off the course in the middle of his first Open at St Andrews in 1921. Or perhaps he was simply behaving like a petulant teenager. Whatever the reason, Tommy quit before the final round, an inglorious moment in one of the most glorious careers in the history of golf.

If Young Tom's game needed seasoning, he could not have had a better training ground than St Andrews in the latter half of the 1860s. His competitors in those days were among the great golfers of the age. Two of them – St Andrews native Jamie Anderson and Musselburgh man Bob Ferguson – would go on to prove that James Denham was a bit optimistic that night at Mr Leslie's when he predicted that Tommy's feat in winning the Belt would never be matched. Both would win three consecutive Opens.

Jamie was the son of David Anderson, a fixture in St Andrews popularly known as 'Old Daw'. He made clubs and balls and, later in his life, ran a popular ginger beer stand on the links. Born in 1842, Jamie was nine years older than Tommy. He was a reticent moustachioed man, inclined to be portly as he aged, and a bit too fond of drink for his health. He approached golf far differently than the game's rising star. He was not about to take the chances Tommy took. Jamie's goal was to make no mistakes. He marched calmly forward, letting his opponents take the risks and pay the price. Gradually, he wore them down with unwavering accuracy and deadly putting.

Harry Everard, the golf historian who was a close friend of Old Tom's and a contemporary of Tommy and his mates, said he once heard Jamie remark 'that he had played 90 consecutive holes without one bad shot or one stroke made otherwise than he had intended, and it was this dead level of steadiness which brought him conspicuously to the front.'

Ferguson, too, could not have been a more different man than Young Tom. On and off the course, Bob was as quiet and unassuming as his rival was bold and confident. Two years Tommy's senior, Bob was a strong, stocky golfer who drove the ball a long way and was deadly with a cleek, the equivalent of a modern two-iron. He had a broad face and wide-set eyes, accented by a thick patch of beard that gave him a quizzical look. Bob's most distinctive characteristic, however, was that in a world of hard-drinking caddies he was a teetotaller. He would become for Tommy what Willie had been for Old Tom: his leading opponent from Musselburgh and thus a fierce rival in professional tournaments and challenge matches.

'When anything had to be done, there was a most valuable ingredient in his composition – sheer downright tenacity of purpose and determination,' Everard wrote in describing Bob's game. 'To see him address the ball was in itself a study; broad-backed and sturdy, it appeared if nothing short of a volcanic upheaval or a dynamite cartridge would have power to make him budge till the stroke was finished.'

Just a notch below Anderson and Ferguson was Bob Kirk, a ball maker who went on to become the golf professional at Blackheath in London. Small and wiry, Bob was six years older than Tommy. He never finished better than second in the Open, although he managed that three times, including that memorable Open Championship when he rode home with the new owner of the Belt. Bob did have three victories in the tournament at St Andrews and was among the few players to beat Tommy one on one. His game was distinguished by two qualities every golfer lusts after. He drove the ball straight and putted beautifully. That made him a tough opponent and valuable teammate for Tommy and his father, who was especially fond of Bob.

Tommy's best friend and chief rival was Davie Strath. Like Tommy, he was an educated man who cut a dashing figure. Tall and regal, with his hair swept straight back from his forehead and often a neatly trimmed moustache, Davie was that rare golfer that bettors were prepared to back against the young prodigy in his prime. Davie's game was as elegant as his looks. His 'style was the very poetry of swing, the most perfectly graceful and easy that can be imagined,' wrote Everard, who considered Davie one of the greatest players St Andrews ever produced. Davie did have one glaring weakness, however. He was a highly strung, fidgety player who sometimes unravelled under pressure. That tended to be his undoing in matches with Tommy.

Then apprenticed as a law clerk, Davie was a descendant of one of St Andrews' great, if ill-fated, golf families. In 1864, his elder brother Andrew had replaced Old Tom as keeper of the green at Prestwick. The following autumn Andrew won his first Open. A second elder brother, George, would play well enough to compete in both the Open Championship and the US Open, having emigrated to America for a successful career teaching golf and designing courses. Only George would live to an old age, dying in New York a few months after his 75th birthday. Andrew played in two more Opens after his victory, but he would not win again or live to see Tommy's breakthrough. In February 1868, at the age of 32, Andrew died of tuberculosis. Years later it would send Davie to an early grave as well.

Tommy and Davie were first pitted against one another in 1866, when Tommy was 15 and Davie was 17. Both had been playing such promising golf that the barons of St Andrews decided to enliven their spring meeting by arranging a match between them. They made a rakish pair those two. While their contemporaries tended to dress like country bumpkins, the young stars favoured a far more modern look. They wore slim-cut suits that they accented with brightly coloured silk ties and gaudy watch chains draped across their vests. Tommy finished his outfit with a black felt hat, not yet having adopted the Glengarry bonnet that would become his signature as a champion. Their clothes weren't the only reason Tommy and Davie stood out. Most of their brethren sported bushy mutton chops or beards as evidence of their manliness. Tommy and Davie were clean-shaven, except perhaps for a tidy moustache. In the Victorian age, as historian Ruth Goodman put it, 'The clean-shaven were the young lovers of the world.'

That first match between Tommy and Davie consisted of two trips around the St Andrews Links, 36 holes in all, played for a healthy stake of £20. With lords and ladies of The R&A following along, Young Tom eked out a narrow victory, a finish so close that it demanded a rematch. An even larger gallery turned out to watch the two rising stars do battle a second time. Davie turned the tables on his young friend by holing a long putt on the final green to even the score at one victory apiece. The debut of Tommy vs Davie was every bit as memorable as the one Old Tom's laddie had made two years earlier when he vanquished William Greig on the North Inch of Perth. Whether they knew it or not, the gentlemen of St Andrews had just inaugurated the rivalry that would one day revolutionise their game.

Impressive as his play could be, Tommy was still very young and there were as many setbacks as successes. He competed in the 1866 Perth Open – which turned out to be the last one

ever held – and finished far back, 18 strokes behind local hero
Bob Andrews. In 1865 and 1866 he played three times in the
tournament for professionals at St Andrews, never finishing
better than fourth. Tommy's second appearance in the Open
wasn't particularly impressive either. He turned in mediocre
scores in all three rounds of the 1866 Open Championship: 63,
60 and 64. That left him nine strokes behind his father and 18
behind the winner, Willie Park. Willie claimed the Belt for a
third time as his brother David finished second.

Golf aside, 1866 was a momentous year for the Morris family.
It was the year Old Tom bought the house and shop at 6 Pilmour
Links, an enormous step up from the small cottage he and his
family of six had occupied since returning from Prestwick. Tom
was probably the first golfer wealthy and connected enough to
own property in an age when nearly all craftsmen were renters.
His stature gave Tommy and every other member of his family
that rare chance to rise above the class into which they were born.

Old Tom paid £400 for the property, borrowing the money
from Thomas Milton, the provost of St Andrews. A leading
member of the Royal & Ancient, Milton sported a bushy
white beard that made him look a little like Santa Claus. The
shop could not have been more ideally situated, located as it
was across from the last green and first tee of the links, with a
view of the sea beyond. Better yet, at least from Nancy Morris's
perspective, the house and shop were separate buildings, with a
small garden between them. For the first time in their lives, Old
Tom and Nancy had a home that wasn't dominated by the noisy
and smelly business of making clubs and balls.

Young Tom turned 16 the following spring and began to
mature into the player who 'quite overshadowed his father's great
reputation as a golfer', as Tom's biographer William Tulloch put
it in that classically understated Victorian way. In the first big
professional tournament of the year, held in May at the historic

Links of Leith near Edinburgh, Tommy finished fourth. He trailed his father by a stroke and was 11 behind the winner, the implacable Bob Ferguson, who took home the winner's share of £10.

The breakthrough came on 19 September 1867 on the treacherous links of Carnoustie just north of the Firth of Tay, a course still considered among the most difficult in the world. There Tommy met the largest and toughest field yet assembled for a professional tournament. Every top player from St Andrews, Prestwick, Musselburgh and Perth was there, 32 in all, competing for a purse of £20, with half to the winner. That was nearly twice as much as the first prize at the Open.

The tournament was a 30-hole affair, three rounds of the ten-hole course laid out by Allan Robertson the year before Tommy was born. It would later be expanded to 18 by his father. For the first time as a professional, Tommy delivered on the promise he had shown as a 12-year-old at Perth. He came in with a score of 140 for the three rounds, brilliant golf for that era. It left him tied for the lead with two of the toughest players in the game, Bob Andrews and Willie Park. The three of them would determine the winner in a one-round play-off.

As always, every golfer and fan on the grounds was reaching into his pocket to bet on the outcome. Given that Tommy had yet to win as a professional and that Willie and Bob were experienced veterans, it is no surprise that they were heavily favoured. Even Tommy's own father didn't back him, thinking his son 'ower young' to stand up to such pressure. The bettors were wrong. Young Tom played astonishing golf in that play-off. He sprinted to an early lead and never let up, finishing the ten holes in 42, a phenomenally low score in those days of rustic clubs and rough-hewn courses. Bob trailed by four and Willie surrendered when he knocked his ball into the Barry Burn.

The crowd cheered Young Tom lustily as he holed out on the

final green, even though most of them had probably lost a pound or two betting against him. Everyone must have realised that they had witnessed something extraordinary. That field of 32 players – the era's equivalent to a modern World Golf Championship – was as deep and talented as any ever assembled. Golf would not see its like for years. And a mere lad of 16 had just taken them down.

The next day, Young Tom reinforced the message that a new star had arisen when a match for £5 was arranged between him and Willie, the reigning Open champion who shared with Old Tom the title of Scotland's King of Clubs. Young Tom humbled him, winning by eight holes up with seven left to play, a beating as severe as any Willie suffered in his distinguished career on the links.

Tommy's ascent was so definitive that when the professionals gathered again a week later at Prestwick to battle for the Belt, it was the first time in the quest for that red-leather trophy that bettors had to worry about someone other than Willie or Old Tom, who had dominated the tournament for the better part of a decade.

In Tom's scrapbook, there is a newspaper clipping that puts it plainly: 'The cognoscenti were in perplexity, not knowing whom to back.' There was no betting favourite in that Open Championship. Any player in the field could be had at odds of 4/1. The reason, as the reporter explained, was that new stars on the scene – namely Young Tom – 'had lately proved themselves dangerous rivals to the most experienced golfers in the kingdom.'

Old Tom won that Open, the fourth and final time he would wear the Belt. His young son finished fourth, five strokes back. But Old Tom must have known by then that he and Willie had seen the last of the days when they would be lords of the Open Championship.

Five

THE GIFT OF GOLF

———————— •●◉●• ————————

No one knew better than Bob Ferguson the intimidating presence Young Tom brought to the golf course during the torrid three-year run that followed his eye-opening victory at Carnoustie.

Bob ran into that unstoppable force one afternoon at Luffness Links just east of Edinburgh. He had never seen the kind of golf Tommy played that day. No one had. Every time Tommy made a putt – at least it seemed as if it were every time – he would look over to his caddie and say, 'Pick it out of the hole, laddie.' With that he would stride confidently off the green, leaving the putt to drop in just as he had predicted.

That was pure Tommy. He played the game with a slashing style unlike anything ever seen. Even the brazen Willie Park was impressed by the way Tommy 'went for everything . . . and swung himself clean off his feet.' The great golfers who had preceded Tommy, men like Allan and Old Tom, favoured an approach to the game captured perfectly by the old Scots word 'pawky'. It means shrewd or cunning, both in wit and strategy, and described the player focused on making prudent shots, manoeuvring the ball carefully around hazards to be certain of a tidy score.

Young Tom tried to tear the golf course apart – and did it with a swaggering bravado that could have rubbed people up the wrong way. But Tommy had that rarest of gifts, a personality so winning that all sins are forgiven. Contemporaries remember his amiable qualities and his cheerful disposition in foursomes, even with gentlemen who played horribly. They tend to forget how his brash behaviour and bold frankness sometimes raised hackles in a class-conscious world.

Tommy's approach to the game was fundamentally different from other players of his age. The only thing he did the same as everyone else was to hold the club in the palm of both hands. It would be a generation before Harry Vardon popularised the overlapping grip most golfers use today. In that age, nearly every leading golfer favoured a smooth, full, sweeping swing made at a leisurely tempo. Not Young Tom. He had a shorter backswing than his contemporaries and a furious follow-through that created a penetrating ball flight ideal for playing in Scotland's windy conditions.

'Tommy was the embodiment of masterful energy,' wrote the Reverend William Proudfoot, who watched him play at St Andrews. 'Every muscle of his well-knit frame seemed summoned into service. He stood well back from the ball, and with a dashing, pressing, forceful style of driving, which seldom failed, sent the ball whizzing on its far and sure flight.'

Tommy paid no attention to the universally accepted notion that it was unwise to press for more on a shot. He went all out on every swing, becoming the forefather of all the power players who dominate professional golf today. When he needed extra distance, he swung even harder, sometimes almost falling forward and often sending his Glengarry bonnet flying into the hands of an adoring fan. The crowd loved it, and so did Tommy.

Tommy came of age at a time when the gutty ball was creating new possibilities for how the game could be played. No player seized them as aggressively as he did. Young Tom's go-for-broke philosophy and his genius for inventing shots was nothing short of revolutionary, setting a new standard of performance that would have to be matched by any player who hoped to compete against him. He was as groundbreaking in his age as Tiger Woods would be in another.

During the feather-ball era, golf had been played almost exclusively with long-nosed wooden clubs. They were made by splicing flexible hickory shafts to thin faces of harder wood like blackthorn or beech. Woods became the clubs of choice for the simple reason that a ball hit with an iron was likely to be reduced to a pile of leather and feathers. Most players used fewer clubs than golfers do today, between six and nine. Their clubs had different names, too. Golfers took their play club when driving from the tee and one of several spoons with more lofted faces for long shots from the fairway or rough.

Even for a short shot to the green over a bunker, players reached for a wood, a quirky club with a steeply lofted face that was called a baffing spoon. The only lofted iron most golfers carried was invented to deal with the reality that links were public areas where workmen in wheeled carts left deep tracks that presented a brutal hazard. Players used their rut iron to extricate balls from such impossible lies. On the green, golfers favoured wooden putters barely distinguishable from their other clubs, although some preferred to putt with a long-shafted, thin-faced iron that came to be known as a cleek.

By the time Tommy made his debut in 1864, the durable gutty ball left players free to discover new ways to use irons. The cleek, for instance, took on a role far beyond putting. It became the club of choice from the tee on short or narrow holes and from the fairway, too. In the hands of a skilled golfer, the cleek could be a deadly accurate weapon, lacing the ball on a rope towards the pin. Golfers must have loved them because when they posed for a portrait, players usually did so holding a cleek. The great British champion Harry Vardon expressed the sentiment best: 'There is no shot in golf which gives greater joy – I am not sure that there is any which affords such complete satisfaction – as a well-hit ball with a cleek.'

Tommy set the tone for this transformation, inventing shots that would forever change the game. He began routinely hitting approaches to the green with his rut iron, taking advantage of its loft to create shots that sailed high and stopped quickly. Allan Robertson had been the first to try this. His swing was so precise – scientific, his admirers liked to say – that he could nip a feathery with an iron and plop it onto the green. Tommy perfected the shot, using his rut iron so deftly and so often that it became the forerunner of the niblick and later the sand wedge.

Tommy also carried a short-shafted, straight-faced iron that he used in approaching particularly rough-hewn greens. Instead of putting from just off the surface, as most players did, Tommy would use his iron to pitch the ball a few feet and let it race into the hole. He had created the bump-and-run shot that is now an essential weapon in links golf. Creative and daring as he was, horrible lies held no fear for Young Tom. He seemed to relish them. Contemporaries marvelled at his powers of recovery, just as golfers of another age would shake their heads at the way Seve Ballesteros of Spain would make miraculous shots when all seemed lost.

It was, however, Tommy's magnificent putting that truly set him apart. On most greens, he used his long-shafted, wooden-headed putter, standing upright with his right foot so close to the ball that those watching feared he might brush up against his toe as he drew the club back. He took great pains over every putt, long or short, and was all but invincible on the green, as

Ferguson attested. 'Any sort of putt appeared to be dead to him,' recalled historian Everard, 'and of the short ones he missed fewer than any player the writer has ever seen.'

In that respect, Tommy could not have been more different from his father, who endured years in which he had the yips and missed makeable putts so often that Tommy would needle him by saying, 'Gin the hole was a yaird nearer him, my fawther wad be a guid putter.' Old Tom's reputation was such that when James Wolfe Murray, a flamboyant member of The R&A, jokingly addressed a letter to the 'Misser of Short Putts, Prestwick', it came directly to the Morrises' front door.

With his hell-bent style and the shots he invented, Young Tom won by laughable margins and posted unheard of scores. By the age of 18, he had equalled the record score of 79 at St Andrews, and in the ensuing years there would be even more remarkable rounds to come. It wasn't simply the scoring that struck fear into the hearts of other golfers. It was Tommy's cocksure attitude – 'Pick it out of the hole, laddie.' Tommy's intensity is palpable in nearly every photo ever taken of him. His is the fierce, almost arrogant stare of a player who never once doubted his supremacy, not even as a boy posing with his elders at Perth. All of this added up to a celebrity status previously unknown in golf, even by his father and Allan.

Tommy came into his own just as professional golf was becoming popular among new fans the gutty had drawn to the game. He was a magnetic star arriving at precisely the right moment, just as Arnold Palmer would be in the 1950s, when he captured the imagination of golfers getting their first televisions. Tommy wasn't the only attraction. His father, Willie, Jamie, Bob and especially Davie were all fan favourites. But have no doubt. It was the gallant superstar that hordes of fans flocked to see – and not just men. Reporters following Tommy took pains to mention how many women pressed close to the action to get a glimpse of their dashing hero. Given that golf was such a male bastion, that speaks volumes about Tommy's drawing power.

Naturally, every young boy growing up in St Andrews wanted to be just like Tommy. They copied his daring new shots and imitated his slashing swing, perhaps trying to make their Glengarry bonnet go sailing off in the process. Among them was a caddie named Andra Kirkaldy. He was just a boy when Tommy started winning championships. Later in life, he would succeed Old Tom as the most beloved golfer in St Andrews. 'I could go on for hours, telling of Tommy's triumphs and singing his praise, for we were all his worshippers,' Kirkaldy recalled in his memoir, *Fifty Years of Golf: My Memories*.

A genuine appreciation of Tommy's game requires an understanding of how much harder golf was in that nascent era. Tommy's clubs were far more difficult to hit than the forgiving drivers and irons that golfers use today. Club faces were about an inch deep, with a sweet spot no bigger than a coin. Iron clubs had no grooves, making precision vastly more difficult to achieve. The gutty ball Tommy played with had to be phenomenally well struck to travel farther than 200 yards, and the rules of the game were far less forgiving then than they are now. Even on the putting green, golfers were not permitted to lift or clean their ball. If another player's ball blocked the path to the hole, that was simply a stymie that golfers had to find a way around or over. The stymie rule remained part of golf until 1952.

The biggest challenge, however, was the links itself. Golf courses in the 1860s were nothing like the lush, manicured greens on which the modern game is played. Fairways were rugged and trimmed only by sheep, although horse-drawn mowers had recently been invented. On many courses, every hole was framed by thick gorse bushes from which recovery was a pipe dream. Bunkers were fearsome hazards, deep sand pits that were full of rabbit holes and footprints. The idea of raking bunkers was in the distant future. Greens were nothing like today's billiard tables and sometimes barely distinguishable from fairways. Even as late as 1920, Willie Park Jr. devoted part of his book on putting to dealing with cupped lies. Tee boxes didn't exist either. St Andrews didn't add teeing grounds until 1875. Players simply teed their ball within a few club lengths of the hole they had just finished.

The state of affairs at Prestwick in 1851, when Old Tom arrived to lay out a proper golf course, vividly illustrates the point. For centuries, Scots had played the game on tight-knit turf along the seaside known as links land. The word links has since become synonymous with golf courses, obscuring its true meaning. It refers to undulating, sandy areas common to the east and west coasts of Scotland that lie between the seashore and land suitable for farming. Links were public spaces, used for anything from strolling along the beach to practising archery. The purpose they turned out to be best suited for was playing golf.

Links featured firm turf and were blessed by nature with hazards ideal for the game – tall, wispy fescue, prickly gorse and small streams, or burns, winding towards the sea. In ancient golf centres like St Andrews, courses had been laid out long ago on the links land. When Old Tom arrived in Prestwick, however, there was no formal golf course. As they had been doing for ages, players simply went out onto the vast links, cut out holes with a knife, and started hitting balls to them.

Playing the brand of golf Tommy established under these conditions makes it easy to understand why nearly every player of his age whose memory is recorded – among them Bob Ferguson, Andra Kirkaldy, and amateurs William Doleman and Leslie Balfour-Melville – were firmly of the opinion that Young Tom was the best player they had ever seen or ever would see. Kirkaldy lived to witness Britain's Great Triumvirate of Harry Vardon, John Henry Taylor and James Braid win 16 Open Championships between them, but was left unmoved.

'I am often asked who was the greatest golfer I have known, and my answer is always the same – Young Tom Morris.' Kirkaldy wrote. 'The younger generation of golfers shake their heads and say, "Surely, Andra, he could not have beaten Harry Vardon, J.H. Taylor, James Braid, Sandy Herd, Abe Mitchell or George Duncan." My reply is that I have seen all the cracks and beaten most of them at odd times, but Young Tom had the gift of golf like no man I ever knew. It is my honest opinion that he was just a golf genius.'

That genius truly came to the fore in 1868. It was the same year that Benjamin Disraeli, darling of the Conservative movement, was serving his first term as Britain's prime minister and American outlaw Jesse James was making a name for himself by robbing banks in broad daylight. Tommy celebrated his 17th birthday that April. A month later, at the spring meeting of The R&A, it became obvious that his game had reached a fearful new level.

Two much-anticipated singles matches were arranged for Tommy against leading golfers from rivals Musselburgh, one against Bob Ferguson and the other against William Dow. Tommy crushed Bob in their two-round match, going six holes up with five to play. William gave him more trouble. Their first match was halved when Tommy uncharacteristically missed a short putt to win on the final green. That meant a rematch the next day, and Tommy gave William a beating as sound as the one he had administered to Bob, winning seven and five. The only time Tommy lost at that meeting was when he played in a foursome with his father, who was not in good form. They lost to Bob and his Musselburgh partner David Park by four holes.

The *Fife Herald* took note. 'Thomas Morris, jun., has not simply distinguished himself by gaining every single-hand match in which he has engaged during this spring meeting, but played such an extraordinary game that made every witness look on in admiring astonishment, and that has installed him in the very first rank of golf at the extremely early age of 17.'

Young Tom had to be brimming with confidence by the time he and his father took the long journey to compete in the Open that September at Prestwick. By now he had replaced the old felt cap with the blue Glengarry bonnet that would forever be his signature. He wore it cocked jauntily to one side, sending a message to anyone who cared to notice that Tommy knew he was coming into his kingdom and feared no man or links.

In the four years since Tommy and his father had moved home to St Andrews, the club Old Tom had helped establish in Prestwick had continued to flourish, as did its annual competition to identify Scotland's Champion Golfer. That season, Tommy and his father would get their first look at the gorgeous stone clubhouse that had replaced the tiny quarters Prestwick formerly occupied at the Red Lion Inn.

The quest for the Belt began on Wednesday 23 September 1868. It was a lovely morning in Ayrshire, with barely a breath of wind, one of those rare days that promised low scores. Nevertheless, the dozen players on hand still had a devilishly difficult golf course to conquer. The 12 holes at Prestwick measured 3,799 yards, equivalent to 5,700 over 18 holes, a stern test in that era. The course unfolded along a stretch of coastline as ideally suited for the game as any in Scotland. Shielded from the Firth of Clyde and its majestic Isle of Arran by mammoth natural sand dunes, the green was blanketed in fescue and criss-crossed by the meandering Pow Burn. Demonstrating his knack for discovering imaginative golf holes in any landscape, Old Tom had crafted a classic Scottish links full of blind shots and dastardly hazards. Horace Hutchinson, the noted golf writer, vividly remembered how the 12-hole course played in Tommy's day, before Prestwick succumbed to the emerging trend and expanded to 18 holes in 1882.

'It went dodging in and out among lofty sandhills,' Hutchinson wrote. 'The holes were, for the most part, out of sight when one took the iron in hand for the approach; for they lay in deep dells among these sandhills, and you lofted over the intervening mountain of sand, and there was all the fascinating excitement, as you climbed to the top of it, of seeing how near to the hole your ball might have happened to roll.'

In 1868 there was no established par for Prestwick, or any other course for that matter. The notion of par, the score a highly skilled golfer would be expected to make on a given hole, would not become part of the game until the end of the century. Modern terms for shooting under par on a hole – birdie for one under, eagle for two under – would develop even later. But the first reference to the concept of par did involve Prestwick. In 1870 William Doleman's brother Alexander wrote an article for a British golf magazine in which he asked Jamie Anderson and Davie Strath what score they thought would represent perfect golf at Prestwick. To explain what he meant, Alexander borrowed a term from the financial markets, par, which described the appropriate price of a share of stock. Jamie and Davie agreed that par for Prestwick was a score of 49.

Young Tom signalled from the outset of the 1868 Open that a new era in golf had arrived. In those days, the first at Prestwick was a mammoth hole known as the Back of the Cardinal. The name came from a gargantuan bunker Old Tom had shored up with discarded railroad ties, a motif that would inspire golf architects of the future like Pete Dye. Prestwick's records put the length of the hole at 578 yards, although in some tournaments it may have played shorter than that. Throughout history there has been debate about whether it should be considered a par five, as Doleman had it, or a par six given the limitations of hickory clubs and gutty balls.

Playing flawlessly, Tommy made a five on that brutal opening hole and went on around the course sticking close to Doleman's par. He came in with a new Open record of 51, giving him a two-stroke lead over Bob Andrews. In eight previous Opens – 24 rounds in all – a score close to Tommy's had been made only twice, a pair of 52s put up by Old Tom and Willie. Scores tended to be closer to 60, often higher. In that first round, for instance, Willie had come in with 58 and Old Tom with 54.

Tommy's record didn't last a round. His father and Willie both eclipsed it on their second trip around the course with brilliant scores of 50, the best either had ever managed in an Open Championship. That gave Old Tom a one-stroke lead over his son, who fell back to earth with a pedestrian 54 of his own. Old Tom's lead would prove fleeting. Young Tom absolutely destroyed Prestwick in his third and final round, going around in 49. It was the first time any golfer had come in below 50 in an Open, a psychological barrier every bit as powerful as breaking 80 at St Andrews.

It is one thing to make such a score in a casual round. Andrew Strath and Old Tom had managed that at Prestwick. Pulling it off under Open Championship pressure is far more difficult. Both record scores for St Andrews at the time, twin 79s by Allan and Tom, were achieved outside the crucible of competition. Tommy's score was also level par by Doleman's reckoning. Scores of level par, even in what clearly were ideal weather conditions, simply did not happen in that early age of golf. Even as late as the first decade of the 20th century, scores of three, four or five over par for a round were considered excellent and usually good enough to win.

Tommy's total of 154 for the three rounds of Prestwick blew away all records for the Open Championship. It was eight strokes better than the previous low, the 162 by Andrew Strath in 1865. It was nine strokes better than his father's best in eight previous appearances, and it was a ridiculous 16 strokes lower than Old Tom's winning score the previous year.

At age 17, Tommy would deposit £25 with the secretary of Prestwick Golf Club and carry that red-leather trophy home to the place where it had resided for so much of his childhood, proudly displayed in the Morrises' living room. He had become – and remains to this day – the youngest golfer to win a major championship. But perhaps best of all was that his father had finished second, three strokes back. It was the first time a father and son had run one-two in the Open, and surely it will be the last.

As he would share with his worshippers years later at Mr Leslie's Golf Inn, Young Tom made his mind up then and there that he alone would be the owner of the Belt, the undisputed Champion Golfer of Scotland. Prodigies see their destiny that way. Bobby Jones came to precisely the same conclusion in 1930. He knew he was predestined to win all four of golf's major championships and become the first and only winner of the Grand Slam. Nothing that happened in the rest of the 1868 golf season suggested Tommy would not achieve the goal he now secretly harboured.

He continued to steamroller every golfer in his path. Tommy won both of the remaining professional tournaments played that season, one at Leven and the other at St Andrews. Tommy was so all-powerful that almost no money was bet on that tournament at the Home of Golf, a rarity in a game that drew its lifeblood from gambling. No one was interested in taking on Tommy, and that was the correct instinct. He came in with a respectable score of 87 to win the event, one stroke ahead of his familiar nemesis Bob Ferguson.

Tommy did stumble in a singles match the following day against his feisty friend Bob Kirk, a contest that was more hyped than the professional tournament itself. Newspapers reported that Tommy was 'indisposed'. Chances are that meant he had celebrated his victory a bit too lustily the night before. Bob won the two-round affair by going six holes up with four to play, no doubt costing Tommy's backers a bundle. The champion did not go down without a flash of brilliance, however. In the second round, facing certain defeat, Tommy raced through the first eight holes at St Andrews in the absurd score of 33.

The *Fife Herald* again was impressed. 'Young Tom has won the first prizes at Prestwick, Leven and St Andrews this year, and is playing most beautifully,' the newspaper enthused. Magnificent as his game was, Tommy was not close to playing his best.

Six

DASHING NEW BREED

T ommy was now the youngest Champion Golfer Scotland had ever known. Allan was nearly 30 before he was declared King of Clubs, Tommy's father older still. It wasn't simply his age or his extraordinary gift for golf that set Tommy apart, however. He was unlike any other man in the ranks of professionals. He was educated, forward-thinking and never shy about standing up for himself. He could not have been more different from his brethren, and no one was more aware of that than Tommy himself.

Before he came along, professional golfer meant one of three things – caddie, club and ball maker or keeper of the green. Most men in these trades eked out a meagre existence. The best job was the one occupied by Tommy's father. A greenkeeper earned a comfortable salary and as undisputed authority on golf at his club enjoyed a certain social status among gentlemen. Slightly less exalted were men like Willie Park, who ran their own club- and ball-making shops. Below them were their craftsmen, men like Bob Kirk and Jamie Anderson. Working in the shop gave all of them the flexibility to pad their bankrolls by serving as a gentleman's caddie or partner in money matches. The lowest of the low were the motley crew of men and boys who hauled clubs for a few shillings a day.

Whatever their position, professionals were nothing more than servants for gentlemen. They tended their greens with barrow and spade, crafted their equipment by hand, carried their clubs under one arm during a round, and bent over to tee their ball on a mound of sand for every drive. Golf bags and wooden tees wouldn't come along until the turn of the century. What defined a professional's status most vividly, however, was this: if a gentleman needed him as a partner or a caddie, a professional was expected to drop whatever he was doing and head for the links. Professionals rarely minded because it was a chance to make money, although they were no more guaranteed a good payday than a waiter working tables.

It was a curious relationship. Nineteenth-century golfers had contempt for professionals. Not men like Old Tom, of course, but run-of-the mill caddies and ball makers. 'The professional, as we are now chiefly acquainted with him, is a feckless, reckless creature,' sneered British amateur Hutchinson. 'In the golfing season, in Scotland, he makes his money all day and spends it all night. His sole loves are golf and whisky.'

Caddies might have resented that bit about being feckless, if they knew what that word meant, but they would never have denied that their first loves were a good game and a wee nip. Andra Kirkaldy, the charming rogue who got his start carrying clubs, tells an amusing tale in his memoir about a competition for caddies in which the prize for first place was a turkey and the prize for second place was a bottle of whisky. 'Two brothers were in the final,' he recalled, 'and one of them could have won with a five at the last hole. But he deliberately took seven and remarked as he left the green, "Jock can have the turkey, the bottle o' whisky's mair in my line."'

Caddies knew gentlemen considered them beneath contempt, but both men were also aware of a fundamental truth. The caddie was nearly always the better golfer, especially in Tommy's day. Caddies seldom missed a chance to rub that in, as St Andrews veteran Bobby Greig did the day he squired a hapless gentleman around the links. After nine holes, Kirkaldy wrote, the man turned to Greig and asked if he'd kept score. 'No,' the caddie replied, 'but I've kept coont o' the pieces of turf ye've cut, an' I've put back 165, sir.'

Young Tom didn't fit neatly into any of the categories that defined a professional golfer. He had a radically different idea of his place in the world than those men did. His schooling at Ayr Academy left him keenly aware that the world was changing all around him. Self-improvement was the watchword of his age, preached even from the pulpit on Sundays. Not for a minute would Tommy have accepted the notion that being born to the artisan class made him inferior to the gentlemen he played with in foursomes. He would never have been openly disrespectful to a club member – his father made a living serving them – but he kowtowed to no man and everyone in St Andrews knew it.

Unlike every other professional golfer of his time, his father included, there is no evidence that Tommy ever caddied. He could not have imagined himself carrying another man's clubs or stooping to tee up his ball. Watching Old Tom do it must have made him cringe. Tommy no doubt worked occasionally in his father's shop, especially when he was young. There is a picture of his locker that shows club-making tools on the shelf, and when asked for his occupation on official documents Tommy described himself as a golf ball maker. That may have been because there was no category for the life he actually lived, earning his keep by playing the game.

Once he started winning professional tournaments and high-stakes challenge matches – and that was happening long before he came of age – Tommy can't have done much else. In the Victorian era, every family member's job was to earn as much as possible. There was simply too much money to be won on the golf course for Tommy to have spent his time in the family's shop fashioning clubs and balls. His brothers and Old Tom's other workmen could take care of that.

Young Tom represented a dashing new breed of professional golfer. His first victory in the Open and the glories that followed gave him the leverage to establish a fundamentally different relationship with gentlemen. When called upon to compete in foursomes, Tommy's fellow professionals simply showed up at the links and accepted whatever reward their patron provided. They wouldn't get much if their side lost. Tommy wouldn't play by those rules. Gentlemen who backed him in challenge matches or took him as a foursome partner understood that Scotland's undisputed King of Clubs had to be rewarded handsomely, win or lose. These agreements may have been unspoken; Victorian men did not openly discuss money. But Tommy had a price, and gentlemen paid it, happily or not, knowing that with the young champion on their side they were all but certain to prevail.

Tommy's insistence on setting his own terms might easily be chalked up to a champion asserting his privilege. But in a society as conscious of class as Victorian Scotland it was far more than that. He had taken the bold first step on the road to equality for professional golfers. Young Tom's rejection of the status quo made a statement that the day was coming when no ball maker in the shop, no caddie in the yard, no golfer who called himself a professional, would consider himself the servant of any man.

Tommy had chummy relationships with many of the gentlemen he knew, men like R.J.B. Tait of the famed East Lothian golfing family. Tait remembers sharing a hotel room with Young Tom during one of the superstar's visits to Luffness. They spent the evenings playing iron shots for pennies from the hearth-rug into a hat sitting on a bed. Tommy, of course, would not live to see his brethren treated as peers of the gentlemen they squired in matches. Even Old Tom, revered as he was, set foot in The R&A's clubhouse only when attending meetings of the Green Committee. Otherwise, when he wanted to speak to a member he tapped on the window to get someone's attention. It would be half a century before a golfer as flamboyant as Tommy came along to pick up the mantle of social equality and bull his way into the game's inner sanctums.

In 1920, when American star Walter Hagen showed up in England for his first Open at Deal, he resented the pernickety way he was informed that professionals were not allowed to change into their golf shoes in the gentlemen's clubhouse. The reigning US Open champion responded as only he could. He pulled his rented Austin-Daimler limousine, complete with chauffeur and liveried footman, into the clubhouse driveway and started changing there. If he had a late tee time, he would add to the show by having his footman serve him lunch on the running board. The message had been sent. Later that summer, when the US Open was held at the Inverness Club, Ohio, professionals were welcomed into the clubhouse for the first time, and soon the barriers dropped everywhere.

Whatever gentlemen thought of Tommy and his fellow professionals, even they would have been forced to acknowledge that his plan to make a living by playing the game was working out beautifully. Winning the Belt for the first time in 1868 earned Tommy £6. Over the next two weeks, he won another five at Leven and eight more at St Andrews. In one month, a mere teenager had taken in £19. That doesn't include anything Tommy made from foursomes with gentlemen or side bets on his tournaments and matches.

Some perspective on Tommy's income is provided by comparing his earnings to those of an average Scotsman. In

1867, the year Tommy had his breakthrough win at Carnoustie, seven of ten working Scots had incomes of less than £30 a year. Skilled workers might earn up to £50, the salary Old Tom was earning as the keeper of the green at St Andrews. Young Tom could make an average man's annual wages in a few months. The years ahead would prove that was a mere pittance compared to the amount the young superstar was capable of earning at golf.

The money his best friend was making encouraged Davie Strath to stake his future on a professional golf career. Davie was in an entirely different position to Young Tom. He occupied a nebulous world between professional and gentleman. Davie's apprenticeship as a law clerk did not leave him free to drop everything to caddie or play as a gentleman's partner. In that way at least, he did not fit the age's definition of a professional golfer. More importantly, if his job at the law office led to work as a barrister, Davie might harbour faint hopes of being welcomed into a club for gentlemen, even though he had been born into the working class.

When St Andrews held its tournament for professionals in October 1868, less than a month after Tommy's first victory in the Open, Davie knew he faced a choice. If he entered, any dream of prising open the clubhouse door would be dashed. That was made clear the day before the event, when a committee of The R&A dispatched two prominent members to warn Davie that if he played he would be forever after considered a professional. Davie could see that his best friend was changing the equation for professionals and making a bundle of money in the process. He couldn't resist the temptation. Davie cast his lot with Tommy by entering that tournament – a decision the *Fifeshire Journal* called foolish – and before a year had passed he had quit his job at the law office to play golf full-time.

Just as it took decades for professionals to gain entrance into gentlemen's clubhouses, it would be generations before it became routine for golfers to earn a living solely by playing the game. Even the great Hagen, who made a small fortune in tournaments and exhibition matches, kept a side job as a club professional. But Tommy was charting the path to a future in which golfers would play the sport they love and make themselves rich in the process. He was finishing what had been started by men like his father, Allan and Willie. He was emerging as the first truly professional golfer, as we understand the meaning of that word today.

Young Tom's unwillingness to adhere to social conventions the way his father did – Old Tom was beloved partly because he always knew his place – did not go unnoticed in St Andrews. Gentlemen of The R&A didn't care for Tommy's habit of behaving as if he were the equal of men far above his station. They considered the young champion a bit full of himself. But he was a superstar – their superstar – and in every era men have tended to overlook the shortcomings of their sports heroes. No matter what he did, Tommy remained a beloved figure in St Andrews and wherever golf was played. If time would prove anything, it was that.

It is hardly surprising, given the age in which he grew up and his schooling, that Tommy and his closest friends were not prepared to accept a status quo that granted landed gentry all of society's rights and privileges. Three years before he was born, in 1848, Britain saw the launch of the Chartist Movement, which took its name from a charter outlining changes the reformers sought. Every one of them was aimed at weakening the power of the gentry while strengthening the growing working class created by the Industrial Revolution. Chartists wanted every man 21 or older to have the right to vote, not just those who owned property. They wanted Parliament to be open to any person, not just those with land and money. To make that feasible, they wanted positions in Parliament to carry a salary.

By the time Tommy reached his mid-teens, that movement

had resulted in the Representation of the People Act of 1867, a pivotal change that extended the right to vote to a large segment of the working class. The number of eligible voters in England increased from just over one million to just over two million, and broader suffrage over time became an inevitability. Two years later, the reforms were extended to Scotland. Tommy, Davie and their educated friends would have followed these public debates intently.

In February 1868, seven months before his first Open victory, Tommy and Davie were key players in forming a social club of their own. The town already had a club for those who could not dream of joining The R&A – The St Andrews Mechanics' Golf Club, whose members were mainly local businessmen or traders. Many were men like Old Tom, who had received minimal schooling, read only the Bible and struggled to write. The members of this new club were different. They were, principally, the more educated young men in town, among them students of Madras College. The name they chose for their club speaks volumes: The Rose Golf Club of St Andrews. The rose is the national symbol of England, in Tommy's day ruler of the proverbial Empire on which the sun never set and the home to all that was new and progressive. These were forward-looking men with ideas for the future. They met regularly in local pubs to hash over the issues of the day and no doubt to chatter about the men who considered themselves their betters.

Debating issues wasn't The Rose Club's only business, however. Golf was on the agenda too, especially matches between two members who happened to be emerging as the game's brightest stars, Tommy and Davie. Their rivalry had been building since that spring three seasons ago when the gentlemen of The R&A arranged that first match between them. It only picked up steam when Davie quit his job and turned professional. Tommy and Davie had not yet become golf's most riveting attraction. That title was still held by the 'First Family of Golf', Young Tom and his father, but the day was fast arriving when battles between the two stalwarts of The Rose Club would dominate and transform the game.

The turning point may have been The R&A's spring meeting of 1869. The marquee professional event of that meeting was supposed to be a foursome in which Old Tom and his son took on Bob Ferguson and David Park for £50 a side. As always when a match involved men from St Andrews and Musselburgh, a fervent crowd turned out to follow the golfers around the links. The St Andrews faithful had to be dismayed by what they saw. Father and son were humbled on their home course. Bob and David cruised to an easy victory, closing out Tommy and his father on the 16th by going three holes up with only two to play. It wasn't a surprising loss. Old Tom was badly off form, as he would be all year. A few months earlier, he and Tommy had been drubbed in a foursome by another Musselburgh duo, Ferguson and Willie Park.

Their pride no doubt wounded, the gentlemen of St Andrews turned to Tommy and Davie to avenge the embarrassing defeat. They would take on Bob and David in a rematch of sorts, with another £50 riding on the outcome. Tommy and Davie dispatched the Musselburgh duo so easily that it left every golf fan hungry for more from these young friends and rivals. Money men never miss an opportunity like that. They arranged a match between Tommy and Davie that became the most talked-about event that spring in the old, grey town, as all of their clashes would be in the years ahead. Bettors wagered lavishly on the outcome, with most of the money going on Tommy. The game's reigning champion rewarded his backers, winning by four holes, as well as he would do in any of his matches against Davie.

Avenging losses was something of a theme for Tommy in 1869. Earlier that year, he'd taken on the job of exacting retribution for the most humiliating defeat his father had ever suffered – losing six straight matches to Ferguson, all by enormous margins. Tommy defended his father's honour by challenging Bob to a match over three courses. They played two rounds at each man's home course, St Andrews and Musselburgh, with the deciding rounds at Luffness Links, east of Edinburgh.

Tommy won at St Andrews and Bob evened the score at Musselburgh. The crowning blow came at Luffness. That was the match Bob remembered all his life as the day he confronted the game's most intimidating golfer. It consisted of two trips around the course's 17 holes. In the opening round, Tommy dropped putt after amazing putt and raced out to a six-hole lead. 'Before the match was half over, it had almost become a foregone conclusion,' *The Haddingtonshire Courier* reported. That turned out to be true. Tommy embarrassed Bob as badly as the Musselburgh man had his father. He closed out the match early, going eight holes up with seven still to play. Three decades later, Bob was still shaking his head in amazement as he shared the story of that day with his friend and author George Colville.

As the summer of 1869 wound down, with the Open around the corner, Young Tom continued to display exquisite form. Twice that season he went around the St Andrews Links in 79, a record score that had been made only three times in more than 400 years of golf over that hallowed course. Allan was the first to do it, in September 1858, one of the greatest rounds of all time given the narrowness of the course in those days and the primitive condition of the greens. Old Tom followed suit in 1866, going out in 36 and coming home in 43. Tom's front nine was considered the finest golf seen up to that date at St Andrews. Weeks before Tommy made his first 79, his friend Jamie Anderson had gone around in the same score.

When 14 players gathered on 16 September 1869 to compete for the Belt, two regulars were conspicuously absent – Bob

Andrews and Willie Park, who missed his first Open since the Championship was instituted. Perhaps they were ill. Perhaps they had a conflict no one bothered to record. Or perhaps they decided, as many did, that there was no point in wasting money travelling to Prestwick, given the way Young Tom was playing. In addition to the two 79s, Tommy had swept the prizes at tournaments in Burntisland and North Berwick. If Willie and Bob were intimidated, Davie and Jamie were not. The St Andrews men both entered the Open for the first time that year.

The morning of the Championship dawned brilliantly clear, but a strong north-west wind was blowing across the links and it would prove meddlesome all afternoon. Oddsmakers installed Tommy as the 2/1 favourite to win the Open for the second year in a row, and hundreds of fans poured onto the course to watch him. 'The excitement over the match was widespread,' the *Fife Herald* reported. 'The Links was dotted over with expectant parties, who watched the game with the greatest interest. Each pair had its accompanying backers, but by far the largest party attended the young champion.'

If rivals like Jamie and Davie had designs on taking the Belt from Tommy, he made it clear in the first round that they had better bring their best game. The eighth at Prestwick, the Station Hole, was played over an intimidating sand dune so tall it was nicknamed the Alps and a bunker so large it was known as the Sahara. At 166 yards, professionals harboured hopes of making a three, but given the hole's dangers, any score was possible. The previous year Tommy had made a three only once in three trips around the course.

This time Tommy holed his shot from the tee, no doubt sending the horde following him into a frenzy. Nothing like that had ever happened in a professional tournament. It was such a shocking development that the correspondent for the *Ayr Advertiser* barely knew how to describe for his readers what Young Tom had accomplished. 'Curiously,' he wrote, 'the Station Hole was made by him in one stroke.' Years later, of course, Tommy's shot would be known the world over as one of golf's rarest feats – the hole-in-one. Tommy finished the first round with a score of 50, just one stroke higher than the record he had set the previous autumn, despite the blustery weather. Reporters following the match – and most of the spectators too – concluded that the Open would end just as it had last year, with Tommy triumphant.

The young champion had jumped out to a three-stroke lead over Bob Kirk and Davie. Golf is a fickle game, however, and no one would have predicted what happened in the second round. Tommy stumbled, at least by his own standards, with an uninspiring score of 55. That was higher than any of his rounds in 1868. It included an atrocious seven on the 448-yard fourth, a hole known as The Wall because it was backed by an ancient stone dyke that marked the boundary of the links. With a score that high, Tommy could easily have lost his lead. But Davie and Bob had done worse. Davie came in with 56 and Bob 58, Bob having dropped four strokes when he was hopelessly mired in a bunker. Now, Tommy led by four strokes with just a dozen holes to go.

Tommy snuffed out all hope for his competitors in the third and final round. For only the second time in his quest for the Belt, he went around that difficult links without making a single score higher than five, near-perfect golf in that era. His 52 for that final loop gave him a total of 157. That was only three strokes higher than the record he had set the previous autumn, despite having played every round in a fierce wind.

Kirk trailed in second by a staggering 11 strokes at 168. He must have been one frustrated and awed golfer. Bob had made a two on four of his 36 holes, absurdly great golf in 1869. His final score would have been good enough to win a third of the Opens played to that point. Yet he trailed by an enormous margin. Davie finished third, a stroke behind Bob. As was so often the case, he was undone by nerves. On each of the last six greens, Davie missed putts of less than a yard, giving him a miserable 60 in the Championship's third and final round. Poor Old Tom, still off his feed, staggered in at 176, an ugly 19 strokes behind his son.

The question now was not whether anyone other than Young Tom could stake a claim to being the nation's Champion Golfer, but what more could be expected from the 18-year-old who had seized the game by its throat in just two years?

1870

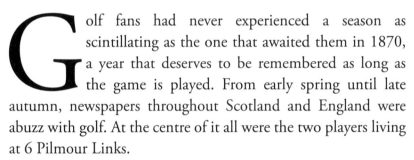

Golf fans had never experienced a season as scintillating as the one that awaited them in 1870, a year that deserves to be remembered as long as the game is played. From early spring until late autumn, newspapers throughout Scotland and England were abuzz with golf. At the centre of it all were the two players living at 6 Pilmour Links.

Every golf fan in the kingdom knew that come September, ownership of the Belt would be on the line for only the second time in a decade. Old Tom had his chance to win it back in 1863, having taken the two previous Opens, but he'd been thwarted by his nemesis, Willie Park. Betting men were ready to risk every pound in their pockets that Young Tom would succeed where his father had failed. They could not have been more sure of it than Tommy was. Ever since he first wrapped the Belt around his waist two Septembers ago, Tommy had foreseen the outcome of the 1870 golf season. He would travel again to Prestwick, claim the game's most coveted trophy, and carry it home to St Andrews in triumph.

But Tommy was not the only golfer facing a momentous challenge that season. His father was preparing for the match of his life, a chance to square accounts with the man who denied him the Belt all those years ago. Gamblers in St Andrews had put up money for Old Tom to challenge Willie Park to another 'Great Match' for £100 a side.

Willie Park had prevailed in their first two clashes, in 1856 and 1858, inspiring a generation of golfers like Bob Ferguson. The young caddie never forgot the thrill of watching his idol carry the day for Musselburgh. Tom got his revenge in 1868. Now he would have a chance to even the score. Like their previous Great Matches, this would be a marathon. They would play 36 holes each over St Andrews, Prestwick, North Berwick and Musselburgh, 144 holes in all. It was, by far, the most talked-and written-about event of the 1870 season, partly because of the heated controversy that erupted in the match's finale.

Old Tom took the match more seriously than he had any competition in his life. He knew he had a significant age gap to overcome. He was a dozen years older than Willie. Tom trained religiously in the months leading up to the match, going as far as to stop smoking the pipe that had been his constant companion since Colonel Fairlie got him hooked on the habit in their early days together at Prestwick. He and Tommy must have spent many an evening discussing strategy by the Morris family's fireside, as always in the company of the Belt. By then it had become something of a family heirloom.

The match began on 14 April 1870, no doubt with Tommy and his Rose Club mates among the throng following every shot. Old Tom got off to a stumbling start on his home course. He fought from behind all morning at St Andrews, falling three holes down by the time they reached the sixth. He battled back gamely, and as they came to the 17th, the famed Road Hole, the match was all square again. Willie hit a brilliant approach shot to that devilish green. Tom's sailed long, into unspeakable trouble, and the match slipped away from him. Willie won by a hole. At Prestwick, the links Old Tom had designed himself and tended lovingly for 14 years, the pride of St Andrews found his game again. Old Tom won by two holes that day and took a one-up lead in the Great Match.

Willie and Tom played their most brilliant 36 holes of the contest at North Berwick, where Scots love to enjoy holidays by the sea. They fought to a draw in that round, setting the stage for a dramatic finish at Willie's home course in Musselburgh. Old Tom still clung to his one-hole lead. The morning of the finale, Friday 22 April 1870, saw the kind of weather for which Scottish golf is infamous, as a gusty south-west wind and lashing rain battered the course. That didn't stop more than 6,000 spectators from showing up. The vast majority of them were rabid Park fans, and they were restless from the outset. Tom and Willie would make four trips around the venerable nine-hole links at Musselburgh to settle matters.

Old Tom won the first nine one up, giving him a two-hole lead in the match and ratcheting up the tension in the partisan crowd. The second nine did nothing to reassure Willie's faithful. It was halved. Park fans had to wait out the lunch break before their man took back a hole by winning the third nine. That left Willie exactly where he had been to start the morning, one down. But now there were only nine holes remaining and the crowd grew increasingly agitated about the outcome as the fourth and final loop began.

Willie won the second hole of that nine – squaring the match – and then seized the lead when the famed 'misser of short putts' did just that on the third green. It was at moments like this that Young Tom wanted to growl at his father: 'The hole'll no' come to you: be up!' Old Tom's miss elicited thunderous applause from raucous Park fans who could not be controlled by umpire

Robert Chambers Jr. From the start, Tom had been heckled and hemmed in, making it all but impossible for him to make an unimpeded swing.

'It is a matter for regret . . . that the onlookers behaved in the most disgraceful manner,' according to a contemporary account reproduced in Tulloch's biography. 'Very fair order was maintained during the first two rounds of the links; but as the crowd increased and the excitement over the result intensified, the players were pressed in upon in a very rude manner and were scarcely allowed room to use their clubs freely.'

Before the players arrived at the fourth hole, Chambers decided the crowd was too unruly for play to continue, as fans showed no respect for the gallery rope that officials had brought out to restrain them. 'Notwithstanding all exertions, no means was practicable for keeping back the onlookers, some of whom by their conduct rendered fair play an impossibility,' he said. Chambers postponed the final six holes until 11 o'clock the next morning, with hopes that a cooling-off period would settle the crowd.

Willie refused to accept that decision. He marched out of Mrs. Foreman's, the pub both players had ducked into when Chambers halted the match, and straight to the fourth tee. With the rowdy mob in tow, Willie played out the final six holes by himself. He came in with 22, absolutely magnificent scoring for that stretch of golf. Willie promptly sent a letter to Robert Dudgeon – the man entrusted with holding the £100 put up by each side before the contest began – declaring himself winner of the Great Match and demanding the money. Dudgeon ignored him.

Old Tom and Chambers dutifully showed up on Saturday morning, and Tom finished those same six holes in a pedestrian 28. Park fans booed loudly as he holed out on the final green. Chambers issued his decree: 'As referee in the match between

Morris and Park on 22 April, and in terms of my decision, the remaining six holes were played by Morris this day, Park declining to finish the game. I therefore declare Morris to be the winner, R. Chambers Jr., Musselburgh, 23 April 1870.'

That would not prove to be the final word either. By 20 May, the *Dundee Courier* was reporting that the dispute was headed to the Court of Session at the insistence of the ever-irascible Willie. An arbitrator eventually settled the matter by voiding the match, leaving accounts unsettled between the two titans of golf's formative years. Tom and Willie would not have another marathon match until 1882, when the Grand Old Man of St Andrews was in his sixties. He won easily that time, which must have been salve on the wound left by the ignominious conclusion of that match in 1870.

With his father's big moment behind him, it was time for Young Tom to concentrate on the challenge he would face come September. Confident as he was in the outcome of the 1870 Open, Tommy spared no effort in sharpening his game. He trained every bit as hard as his father had, travelling more than ever that year. Two weeks after his father's match against Willie, Tommy got every golf fan in Scotland salivating in anticipation of the autumn classic at Prestwick when he made it vividly clear that nothing had changed atop the pecking order of professional golf since his dominant win there eight months earlier.

He and a field of the game's leading players competed on 3 May in the professional tournament at St Andrews, playing one round over the links. Young Tom and Bob Ferguson tied at 86 apiece at the end of regulation. They went another 18 holes to play off the tie and, remarkably, again came in with matching 86s. Then came the explosion. In the second play-off round, Tommy sprinted through the first nine in 37, just a stroke behind his father's legendary 36 in 1866. He went around the home nine in 40, for a score of 77. Newspapers promptly declared it the best round ever played at the Home of Golf. 'This score of Tom's has never been equalled on the St Andrews Links, 79 being the nearest approach to it, and that has been accomplished but seldom,' said the *Dundee Advertiser.*

Tommy's friend Jamie Anderson begged to differ. On 19 August 1869, he had gone around that storied links in 77 himself, an accomplishment that hadn't garnered much attention because his score wasn't made in a tournament and he wasn't Tom Morris Jr. Miffed at the slight, Jamie wrote a letter to the editor of the *Fifeshire Journal* to remind everyone in golf who had set the record at St Andrews.

A month after posting that record-equalling score, with reporters following his every step, Tommy was off on a training tour of England, where he would play at Westward Ho! in North Devon, Blackheath in London, and Royal Liverpool on the north-west coast. At Westward Ho! three matches were staged for the entertainment of golf fans. They featured the two-time Open champion as the star, along with Bob Kirk and Tommy's boyhood friend from Prestwick, Johnny Allan, then the golf professional at North Devon.

The matches were contested over a links that must have reminded Tommy of his childhood home. With its towering sand dunes, Westward Ho! was a spiritual cousin to Prestwick, characterised by unforgiving hazards that brutally punished any shot imperfectly played. When Tommy and Bob Kirk teed off for their match, they sent their drives sailing into a boisterous north-west wind as light rain doused the links. One of the newspaper reporters on hand followed them around and recorded every shot. The clipping, preserved in Old Tom's scrapbook, provides a fascinating insight into how exasperating it must have been to compete against Tommy at the peak of his powers.

Tommy and Bob had played against one another countless times: at the Open, in the professional tournament at St

Andrews, and in singles and foursomes. Kirk knew painfully well how Tommy could overwhelm an opponent. But this had to be an afternoon as humbling for him as that memorable match at Luffness had been for Bob Ferguson.

Tommy was absolutely relentless. After the first hole was halved in fives, he hit a perfect drive from the second tee. It stopped just short of a bunker 90 yards in front of the green. His second shot sailed directly at the flag. When he and Bob Kirk walked up to the green, they found Tommy's ball at the bottom of the cup, the modern equivalent of an eagle. Having seized the lead, Tommy strolled through the next three holes making easy fours. Bob, meanwhile, lipped out a putt to miss a half on the third, got into desperate trouble and made eight on the fourth, and failed to get up and down from a bunker on the fifth, finding himself four holes behind after only five had been played.

What must have been most maddening, however, was Tommy's ability to extricate himself from seemingly insurmountable trouble. On the sixth, he gave Bob a ray of hope when his tee shot was badly bunkered beside the green. But an 'excellent iron stroke' and a 'brisk putt' halved the hole in three. Even when Bob won holes, Tommy made him work for it. On the 11th Tommy foozled another one into a bunker and wound up with a six. But he holed a 15-footer to make Bob earn the win with his putt for five.

In the 15 holes played before Tommy closed Bob out by going four up with only three holes left to play, the champion gave up only one, the 13th. Having failed in a bold attempt to cross a bunker between the tee and green, Tommy compounded his mistake by leaving his second shot in the trap. He had to blast out sideways with his third, and then topped his fourth shot across the green into another bunker. The greatest golfer in the world ended up making an embarrassing eight.

Maybe that is why the reporter who followed the match wrote this in his preamble: 'I proceed to record these matches as I took them down to the best of my ability, anxious to do honour to the brave, and rejoicing over no man's griefs – with the exception that a professional's trials and failures always afford some comfort to the suffering and afflictions of the amateur, buried in bunkers or rushes, and awfully punished.'

The extensive press coverage Young Tom was receiving, along with the determination of fellow professionals not to let him carry off the Belt without a fight, accounted for the robust field of 18 players that assembled for the Open at Prestwick on Thursday 15 September 1870.

A lot had happened in the world during the decade-long quest for that Belt. The Civil War that had been brewing in America when Fairlie launched the Open in 1860 had begun and ended, Lincoln had been assassinated, and in March, Texas had become the last state readmitted to the Union. The British Empire had endured the financial collapse of 1866, which occurred as Karl Marx was scribbling away on *Das Kapital*. It had also reaped the rewards of discovering diamonds in South Africa and opening the Suez Canal. A month before the Championship, the world's first underground railway, the Tower Subway, opened in London. That mind-boggling triumph of engineering undoubtedly was much discussed by Tommy and his friends in the Rose Club.

It had been a monumental year in British sport too. A month before the match between Old Tom and Willie, on Saturday 5 March, the attention of sportsmen had been riveted on the first international football match between Scotland and England, a precursor of today's World Cup. The game was played in London at a 20,000-seat stadium called The Oval. The hearts of Scotsmen in the crowd must have been racing when their boys took the lead in the second half, only to see international glory slip from their grasp as England rallied to salvage a draw.

The morning that would deliver the year's final great moment in sport, the 1870 Open Championship, could not have been more perfect for golf. 'The weather on Thursday was beautiful, and in every way favourable for playing the ancient and national game,' Henry Farnie reported in the *Fifeshire Journal*. 'There was scarcely any wind, and the heat was tempered by light, fleecy clouds which hid the sun's face.'

An unusually large and restive crowd turned out to watch Tommy pursue his destiny. 'Considerably more than the usual interest in the Belt was manifested this year,' Farnie noted, 'as it was known that Young Tom was in excellent form, while the other players were in equally good play, and all determined to prevent the young champion from permanently retaining the Belt, which he would do if he won it on the present occasion.'

Fans from Prestwick, Glasgow and beyond jammed the fairways along the Cardinal's Nob and other 'coigns of vantage' that provided a sweeping view of the links, Farnie reported. The crowd would have included people from all walks of life. Gentlemen decked out in tailored suits and elaborate waistcoats, accented by bow ties and top hats or bowlers; ladies resplendent in flowing gowns, their corsets cinched tightly at their tiny waists, their hair tucked neatly into fashionable bonnets; plainly dressed farmers and labourers, and perhaps a few roughneck caddies who weren't carrying clubs for a competitor. The Open, after all, was free entertainment. The idea of charging for admission to the Championship was still decades away.

From atop those sandy dunes, with the railway and the rooftops of Prestwick visible in the distance, fans could have watched the action on any number of holes, given the tightly interwoven nature of that Ayrshire links. But the vast majority of them were interested in only one player. 'The favourite, and the player who had the largest following,' Farnie wrote, 'was young Tommie, whose careful and steady play was the theme of general admiration. In fact, he never played better in his life.'

Just as he had done in his second victory in pursuit of the Belt, with his now famous hole-in-one, Tommy gave the multitude following him a memory for all time on the tremendous opening hole at Prestwick. At 578 yards, the Back of the Cardinal was so long that it was difficult to reach the green in three shots with a gutty ball and hickory-shafted clubs. Given that so many players needed four swipes to get home, and that par allows for two putts, historians have debated whether it should be considered a par five or more realistically a par six. In his original estimate of par for the Prestwick links, Alexander Doleman had listed it as a par five.

Young Tom holed his third shot from the fairway, a miraculous swing that ranks with the greatest ever made in tournament golf. Surely, it had no rival until 1935, when Gene Sarazen holed his second on the par-five 15th at the Masters, the famous 'Shot Heard Round the World'. Sarazen's remarkable feat amounted to what modern golfers call an albatross, or three under par. If one accepts the argument that the Back of the Cardinal was a par six, Tommy had made one too. Either way it was a shot for the ages.

The roar Tommy's three elicited from his rabid fans must have echoed through the sandy dells of Prestwick and sent an unmistakable message that Scotland's Champion Golfer remained unconquerable. For players hoping to prevent Tommy from claiming the Belt, it was a psychological blow like the one Bob Kirk had experienced on the second hole at Westward Ho! when Tommy's approach shot found the cup. Just as he had done at North Devon, Tommy never let up after that, going around the links in two under the par score posited by Doleman.

Tommy's score for the opening round was an astounding 47, a new record for Prestwick and the Open. It was the second time in his quest for the Belt that Tommy had started by turning in a record score. His closest pursuer, the scrappy Bob Kirk, played superbly, coming in with 52. But he found himself going into the final 24 holes a full five strokes behind. Davie Strath, in third with 54, had seven to make up. He dug in for the second round coming in with a fabulous 49, which until that morning had been the course record. It was no use. Tommy preserved his five-shot lead with a second round of 51, as Bob made 52 again and dropped into third.

The emotional toll of Tommy's relentless assault surfaced in the final round. Davie limped in with a 58 after coming to grief in the cavernous Cardinal Bunker, as so many golfers would do over the decades. Bob didn't do much better with a 57. Tommy cruised through with 51 again, despite another ugly seven at Prestwick's fourth, The Wall, a hole that had proven to be his master more than once. A lesser golfer might have struggled after that disaster, succumbing to the mounting pressure of winning the Belt. Not Tommy. He immediately righted the ship, playing the final eight holes even to Doleman's par and finishing with a new record score of 149 for 36 holes. He had posted the lowest score in all three rounds and lapped the field by a dozen strokes. Both Bob and Davie finished at 161, with Bob prevailing by four strokes in the play-off for second place. Tommy's margin of victory was the largest since his father's 13-stroke win eight years earlier.

It is worth taking a moment to reflect on Tommy's performance, among the most astonishing in the history of golf's oldest championship. It is true that in Tommy's era, fields were small and the competition not nearly as deep as it is today. But wherever and whenever a golfer plays, he still must conquer that opponent Bobby Jones liked to call 'Old Man Par'. Tommy did that better than any golfer of his age or of ages to come. His score of 149 was never equalled as long as the Open was played over 36 holes – a period of 22 years – despite significant improvements in clubs, balls, agronomy and course conditions.

Tommy's achievement, at the tender age of 19, becomes all the more breathtaking when viewed in another context, the notion of going around the course averaging four shots per hole. Early in the 20th century, that became a popular way for British writers like Bernard Darwin to size up a round. How close had a player come to level fours? It was something of a mythical ideal. No one shot level fours – which, coincidentally, adds up to 72, par on the majority of modern courses.

Tommy's record score of 47 was the first time in the Open – and likely any professional tournament – that a player had achieved that mythical ideal of coming in under fours for a round. He averaged 3.9 strokes over those 12 holes, and his score for the entire tournament was only five over fours. The closest any player would come to that during the Open's 36-hole era was the 11 over fours that Willie Park Jr. turned in at Musselburgh in 1889. No golfer would finish the Open in less than five over fours until the introduction of the Haskell ball just after the turn of the century. The Bounding Billy, as that ball was known, changed the game forever by giving golfers a tremendous leap forward in distance off the tee and from the fairway.

Until the coming of the Haskell, winning scores of double digits over fours were common in the Open. Tommy's feat was not surpassed for nearly 40 years, until another great Scotsman, James Braid, took 291 strokes at the expanded, 18-hole Prestwick course in 1908. That left Braid three over fours, two better than Tommy's total of five over. No one would post a score under fours for a Championship until Bobby Jones went around the Old Course at St Andrews in 285 strokes in 1927, or three under fours. It is fitting that Bobby was the first golfer to accomplish that feat. Before going on to become the father of golf in America, Charles B. Macdonald attended St Andrews University and saw Young Tom play in his heyday. Macdonald always considered Bobby to be Young Tom incarnate.

When the last player had turned in his card on that magical afternoon at Prestwick – with Old Tom finishing a stroke behind Bob and Davie – it was time for the moment that Young Tom had envisioned for himself three years ago, when he first laid down a £25 deposit to bring the Belt home with him to St Andrews. John Hamilton Dalrymple, the tenth Earl of Stair, presented the red-leather trophy, with its sparkling silver buckle, to Scotland's undisputed King of Clubs. Two silver shields had been added for the occasion. One read, 'Tom Morris Jun., Champion Golfer'. The other listed his three victories in the Open and the otherworldly scores he posted.

Old Tom looked on proudly as his eldest son claimed the trophy he had dreamed would be his own. True to his character, the Grand Old Man was happier in Tommy's finest hour than he would have been had he won the Belt himself. He would cherish that moment for the rest of his days. After this victory, there would be no more leaving of deposits. The Belt was Tommy's forever now. He would carry it home to what he must have viewed as its rightful place, the Morris family's living room. Sadly, the man whose vision for the future of professional golf produced this glorious day – Old Tom's mentor and friend Colonel Fairlie – would not live to see the end of that unforgettable year. Fairlie died on 5 December, a loss that must have been an especially painful one for the Morris family.

Not long after he won the 1870 Open, Tommy posed for a portrait wearing his handsome new trophy. He stares into the camera as intently as ever, clean-shaven but for his thin moustache. He wears a stylish suit, with piping on the lapels of the jacket and waistcoat, pinstriped slacks and a flashy silk tie. His signature watch chain is draped from his left breast pocket and attached to one of the buttons on his vest. His left arm, crooked at the elbow, rests jauntily on his hip, drawing the viewer's eye directly to the Belt. It would remain forever the iconic image of the dashing young champion.

The presentation ceremony would not have been over long before the celebration was under way at his father's old haunt, the Red Lion. The revelry would go on into the night, just as the party would two days later back home at Mr Leslie's Golf Inn. It was on that night, as Young Tom basked in the admiration of St Andrews' golfing royalty, that Henry Farnie raised his toast to Old Tom and, perhaps, to Allan, Willie, the brothers Dunn and all the heroes of old. Farnie seems to have understood that what he had witnessed that spring and autumn was the sun setting on their era and rising on a new one.

Few men were better equipped than Farnie to recognise the turning point in a drama, especially one unfolding in golf. The cognoscenti knew him as the author of the game's first instructional book, *The Golfer's Manual*, published in 1857 under the pen name 'A Keen Hand'. The wider world knew him as Henry Brougham Farnie, the famed dramatist and librettist whose bawdy translations of French operettas for the London stage provided competition for the more famous and lasting works of Gilbert and Sullivan.

Farnie could see that stars like Tommy competing in tournaments such as the Open represented the future of the game. He made that plain by laying out a challenge as he concluded his coverage of the 1870 Championship: 'As Young Tom carries off the Belt to St Andrews and retains it,' Farnie wrote, 'a new champion trophy will require to be furnished if a wholesome spirit of emulation is to be kept up among the professional golfers of the country.'

Eight

TOMMY TRANSCENDENT

———————— •◦●◦• ————————

Tommy's triumphant march to claim the Champion's Belt lit a fire in the world of golf.

By the spring of 1871, a prominent amateur golfer named Gilbert Mitchell Innes was calling on his fellow Prestwick members to answer Farnie's challenge with a bigger and better Open that would rotate among the most famous links in Scotland, much like today's Championship. His idea sparked a contentious debate that dragged on longer than anyone would have imagined.

Innes wasn't the only person clamouring to see more of Young Tom. Towns across Scotland began following the lead of Prestwick, St Andrews and Perth by hosting professional tournaments to attract golf's first megastar and his growing army of fans. In the ten years before Tommy won the Belt, there were 14 tournaments for professionals. In the ten years after, that number more than doubled to 35. Before long, even clubs in England were dangling money in front of professional golfers, a surprising development given that the game there was still very much in its infancy.

Tommy was so good for business that the prizes put up to lure him and other top players nearly doubled, too. Average purses rose from just over £12 in the 1860s to just under £24 by the 1870s. Some events paid the winner as much as £15. Half a working man's annual salary could be won in an afternoon. Golf was still decades away from anything like a professional tour, but now it was possible to envision a day when men made a living simply by playing the game.

This surge of interest in professional golf is hardly surprising given the show Young Tom was putting on. During his three-year quest to own the Belt, Tommy entered ten professional tournaments and won eight of them. He was nearly as invincible in matches, winning seven of his nine singles and half of his ten foursomes. In every event, it seemed, he inflamed the crowd with a dramatic flourish. The Open's first hole-in-one. The jaw-dropping three on Prestwick's gargantuan Back of the Cardinal. New scoring records at Prestwick and St Andrews, and the immortal 36 holes in 149 to claim that red-leather trophy as his own.

Tommy's feats dwarfed those of the revered Allan Robertson, hero of the feathery era. It is true that Allan was dominant enough that he had once been barred from a professional tournament at St Andrews to give one of the other caddies or ball makers a chance to win. He was not, however, as some wrote in his obituaries, undefeated on the links. Old Tom had beaten him, and Allan once lost every club he owned in a bet at Perth. The truth is, Allan took such pride in his reputation of invincibility that he jealously guarded it by ducking matches he thought he might lose, most notably repeated challenges from Willie Park. Old Tom knew the score. 'I could cope wi' Allan myself,' he was fond of saying. 'But never wi' Tommy.'

Tommy was emerging as the first golfer to stand astride the game – 'the Goliath of his generation', as historian Everard put it. Over the next five years, Tommy's towering fame and sterling play would generate a level of excitement about golf that could never have been imagined in Allan's day. Reporters from both Scotland and England covered Tommy's every move now. That would have been inconceivable even a decade earlier. The game's profile in the press was higher than it had ever been, and the throngs lining the fairways seemed to swell every time the young champion took the field.

Tommy's ascent set in motion seismic changes in the game that would reverberate decades after he had played his last shot. They would unfold slowly, over years if not decades. But every one of them traces to that magical afternoon when Young Tom wrapped the Belt around his waist and emerged as golf's first transcendent player.

His victory at Prestwick and the proliferation of professional tournaments that followed foretold the end of golf's age of match play. Big-money matches would remain popular throughout Tommy's life, contributing significantly to his own legend. But by the turn of the century, challenge matches would be on their way out. The Open and its offspring had made it clear that tournaments represented the game's future as a spectator sport. Match play would always be a mainstay of golf, in amateur events, in international competitions for professionals, and in friendly wagers at the club. But the passion for thrust and parry that had shaped the game for four centuries would never again have the same iron grip on the imagination of golfers. Golf was evolving into a stroke-play game, the sport we know today.

This cultural shift to stroke play had ramifications of its own. When Tommy was a boy, neither the seafarer nor the mason cared what score he made as long as he won his match. Newspapers lavished the same attention on gentlemen – and only gentlemen – whether they won their club's medal with a score of 93 or 103. The rising popularity of tournaments inexorably shifted the focus to making low scores. Perhaps that was inevitable after Tommy won the Belt with the equivalent of two 18-hole rounds in the mid-70s. In a world where the score mattered, battles between gentlemen were destined to lose their place as the only competitions of consequence in golf. There would never be enough gentlemen who could compete with professionals.

Just before the turn of the century, gentlemen would enjoy halcyon days as they narrowed the scoring gap with professionals, launching their own Amateur Championship and popularising the ideal of the amateur who plays for love and not for money. But even then, the gentlemen's game would produce only three players good enough to beat professionals in the Open. In all of history, only one amateur, Bobby Jones, would earn a place among golf's immortals. Gentlemen golfers would always be the game's guiding force through The Royal and Ancient Golf Club and later The United States Golf Association. But the more popular professional golf became, the more gentlemen's competitions became an afterthought.

Those changes were significant enough for a game that had remained all but frozen in amber for centuries. Yet they paled in comparison to the impact of the attention newspapers were lavishing on Tommy and his fellow professionals. That helped ignite a growth boom that spread the Scottish game to England, America and around the globe. Coverage from the English press was the turning point. London gamblers and the sporting publications that catered to them were first drawn to golf by the Open. Their interest was redoubled by Tommy's scintillating run to win the Belt. Golf began growing rapidly south of the border. In the early 1800s, only two golf clubs existed in England, and even there the game was played mostly by immigrant Scots. By the time Tommy made history at Prestwick, that number had risen to 22. Before the end of the century, there were nearly 1,000 golf clubs in the country.

The definitive proof that Englishmen had fallen in love with golf came in 1878, with the first university match between Oxford and Cambridge. Those pillars of British society were naturally drawn to a game played reverentially by competitors wearing jackets and ties. Their embrace meant golf had secured an unshakable position in England, whose Empire would spread the game around the world. Tommy's friends in the Rose Club played an influential role too, introducing golf to nations where they were posted on business. By the end of the 1880s, clubs had opened in the United States, Ireland, South Africa, India and China.

The changes that followed in Tommy's wake set the pattern for a future in which the game would be driven by once-in-a-lifetime players performing feats no one else had dared imagine. Just as Henry Farnie had sensed, Young Tom was ushering in a new age – the age of the superstar. It would continue for the next century and beyond. Every generation would see the rise of a new King of Clubs whose heroics raised the level of play, drew new acolytes to golf and propelled the game into the future. The procession began at the dawn of the next century with England's Harry Vardon and has continued unabated through the era of Tiger Woods.

In the spring of 1871, however, it would have been tough to convince Tommy's contemporaries that golf would ever see his like again. One true believer was Leslie Balfour-Melville, the promising 16-year-old winner of a competition for young gentlemen that Old Tom had organised at St Andrews the previous autumn. Balfour-Melville's score of 93 would have won the gold medal that adults played for the following day. But he knew there was a vast chasm between that performance and the 77 he had watched Tommy make on the same links the previous spring. That conviction was only reinforced by the young champion's victory to claim the Belt and the marvellous golf he would play in the years just ahead.

Balfour-Melville went on to become one of the great amateur sportsmen of his age or any other. He won golf's Amateur Championship and a dozen medals at St Andrews. He emerged as a superstar in cricket, played on international rugby teams, won titles at tennis and billiards, and excelled as a skater and curler. Balfour-Melville lived to be 83, but he never wavered in his belief that the golf he watched Tommy play would never be surpassed. He was asked once how Tommy compared to Harry Vardon. He replied simply, 'I can't imagine anyone playing better than Tommy did.'

Another who insisted Tommy had no equal was Peter Brodie, a former provost of North Berwick. When Tommy was in town, Brodie was fond of backing him to go around the links in a daringly low score. On one occasion, Tommy was playing so casually, puffing away on his pipe and chatting with friends, that a worried Brodie confronted him mid-round. 'Tom,' he said, 'if you don't take care you are going to lose my money.' A bemused Tommy replied, 'How many strokes have I left to play?' Hearing Brodie's answer, he calmly replied, 'It's all right,' and proceeded to finish with a stroke in hand.

Nobody knew better than the barons of St Andrews that Tommy was now the only show in town. They were angling to make the town and its links a summertime destination for a new middle class hungry for holiday entertainment beyond bathing in the sea. Businessmen began sponsoring golf matches, as gamblers had done for years, featuring the game's hometown star. These summer spectacles were possible because newly invented mechanical mowers kept courses playable all year. Before that, the grass was too unruly in summer for real golf and competitions were confined to spring and autumn, the seasons of the annual club meetings.

Contests featuring Tommy came in every stripe. In 1871, he played a match pitting his score on each hole against the best score of two of his toughest competitors, Davie Strath and Jamie Anderson. Tommy beat them both, a testament to the invincible form he continued to display. So confident was Tommy that every day for a week he offered anyone who cared to bet him that he could go around St Andrews in 83. That was a bold wager, given that scores posted in the annual tournament for professionals there tended to be in the mid-80s or higher. Tommy won the bet for five days in a row. On the sixth day, he gave gamblers a chance to win back some of their money by betting himself to go around in 81, four strokes off his course record. He came in with 80, leaving everyone who bet him shaking their heads and emptying their pockets.

Summertime competitions occasionally took on the flavour of modern made-for-TV events. The oddest spectacle of the summer of 1871 was, without question, Tommy's match against James Wolfe Murray, a member of The Royal Company of Archers, who pitted his bow and arrow against Tommy's clubs. Wolfe Murray was a celebrated character at The R&A, the same trickster who had sent Old Tom a letter addressed simply to the 'Misser of Short Putts, Prestwick'. He played his rounds on a white horse, dismounting for each shot, and always employed two caddies, one to carry his clubs and one to hold the reins while he hit his ball. His prowess with the bow proved too much for Tommy. The young superstar kept pace early, but even a golfer of his calibre could not overcome Wolfe Murray's advantages of distance and accuracy. Tommy wound up losing the match.

Curiosities of this sort weren't as rare as one might think. Some years earlier, Tommy had played a match against Bob Ferguson with both men using only Bob's favourite weapon, a cleek. It said something about Bob that he was invincible with that club. Even Vardon admitted that nothing was tougher to hit. 'The face of the club is shallow and almost straight, and unless the ball is struck absolutely accurately, the result is sure to be unsatisfactory,' he wrote. Years earlier, Bob had beaten his childhood hero Willie in a match using only cleeks. Tommy had suffered the same fate, losing by four holes.

In that summer of 1871, Tommy also partnered Gilbert Mitchell Innes in a marathon match against Davie and Jamie that spanned nearly 600 holes. Tommy and Innes finished eight holes ahead, completing one round in a sparkling 79. Still, Tommy found it exasperating that his partner kept interrupting the proceedings with deer-hunting trips, after which he returned off form. 'I cannot understand Mr Innes,' Tommy fumed, jokingly, 'when he's playing as fine a game as any mortal man ever played, leaving gowf to rin after a wheen stinking beast and then comin' back, no' able to hit a ba'!'

As the 1871 season wound down, one question remained on the table, the issue raised by *Fifeshire Journal* correspondent Henry Farnie in his report on Tommy's victory in 1870 to retire the Belt: What was to become of the Open Championship?

In April, at Prestwick's spring meeting, Innes had put forth a proposal to realise the original vision of Colonel Fairlie by inviting St Andrews and Musselburgh to join in buying a new trophy and having the Open rotate among the leading links of Scotland. It proved to be a controversial notion at a club justly proud of its role in establishing the tournament that would evolve into golf's oldest championship.

Harry Hart, the serious-looking, white-bearded man who ran Prestwick as its secretary, immediately sponsored an amendment to Innes's proposal that would keep things precisely the way they were. Prestwick would buy a new Champion's Belt and host the competition only at its links on the Ayrshire coast. Both the Innes motion and Hart's amendment were put to a vote. The club's minutes show that Innes's vision of the future carried the day by a wide margin. But with the club's secretary in firm opposition – and professional golf not exactly a top priority for other clubs – progress was slow.

The autumn meeting of Prestwick came and went with no Open Championship for the first time in a decade. Tommy stayed busy playing professional golf and the usual big-money foursomes with members of prominent clubs in Scotland and England. He competed in three high-stakes challenge matches that year, winning twice. He also played in four tournaments, winning three of those. Tommy took home top honours during a trip to Hoylake and at both the spring and autumn meetings in St Andrews. In his final tournament of the season, Tommy finished second to Davie Strath at Carnoustie, adding fuel to what was already emerging as the most important rivalry in the game since the one between Old Tom and Willie Park.

Everard, the golf historian, considered it an unfortunate rub of the green for Young Tom that no Open was held in 1871. 'Though perhaps nothing could have added to Tommy's renown as a golfer,' he wrote, 'this has always seemed to the present writer . . . rather hard luck on that incomparable player. There is no reason to suppose that he would not have won the 1871 Championship, had there been a Championship to win.'

As the new year dawned, no one knew when – or whether – Tommy would get another chance.

𝒩ine

DREAM SEASON

———————— •●◉●• ————————

I t is a rare day in St Andrews when the talk of the town is about something other than golf. Saturday 6 January 1872 may have been one such day. That morning, the *St Andrews Citizen* published an article describing a ball as lavish as any the old, grey town had ever seen.

Extravagant balls were nothing new in St Andrews. The social event of every golf season was the gilded party thrown by the gentlemen of The Royal and Ancient Golf Club as the finale of its autumn meeting, the last until the new year.

But this ball wasn't thrown by the lords of The R&A. It was put on by the Rose Club, organised by its superstar, Tommy, and his friend and club president James Conacher. What impressed the *Citizen* – and no doubt everyone else – was this: the ball was a far more glittering affair than the one held by The R&A three months earlier in the same town hall. Nothing like it had ever been seen from the working class.

Every corner of the hall was tastefully draped with scarlet cloth and garlands of evergreen. Hung at centre stage was a collage created to celebrate Tommy's historic victory at Prestwick two years earlier. It featured the famous photograph of him wearing the Belt, surrounded on all sides by oval portraits of Rose Club members and luminaries of golf, among them Old Tom, Bob Kirk, the late Colonel Fairlie, writer Henry Farnie and Davie Strath. On the right side of the stage was the gold medal awarded annually to the champion of the Rose Club. On the left was the one decoration no other ball could have displayed – the Belt itself.

In the adjacent council chamber, guests enjoyed a sumptuous feast supplied by Mr Leslie's Golf Inn and desserts from Mrs Thomson, the confectioner. In the orchestra pit, playing beneath the gorgeous new flag of the Rose Club, was a quadrille band that kept a vibrant young crowd of 100 dancing from nine o'clock until half past four in the morning. 'A gay and brilliant assemblage,' the *Citizen* called it.

What a glorious night it must have been for Young Tom, undisputed champion in a town given over to golf. Gallant, nattily dressed and flush, in that crowd he would have had no equal as the most eligible bachelor, except perhaps his suave friend Davie. It is not hard to imagine the young women in attendance, hoping they would wind up dancing with Tommy when the quadrille band struck up a tune.

It is tantalising to wonder if one of the women there was Margaret Drinnen, the housemaid of a wealthy St Andrews couple who would soon become the love of Tommy's life. No one knows if she attended. It's not even certain if she had moved to St Andrews by then. All that is known is that she arrived in St Andrews sometime after the 1871 census. Still, the ball was as likely a spot as any for the pair to have first spied one another across a room.

The sensation created by the Rose Club ball spoke loudly for Tommy and his friends. It showed everyone in St Andrews –

and those who read about the ball in national newspapers – that these young men had money to spare and tastes every bit as refined as those of gentlemen who could never imagine allowing them entry to The R&A.

One cannot help but wonder how the ball was viewed in a staid, upper-crust town like St Andrews, especially whether Old Tom confronted any ruffled feathers when his employers were greeted by the *Citizen*'s fawning coverage of a ball whose opulence had dwarfed their own. If R&A members had any reaction beyond a raised eyebrow, it remains to be discovered.

It is easy to understand why Tommy was in a celebratory mood. His game was more dominant than ever, and he was watching his dream life unfold as he prepared for a golf season that would rival any seen in the centuries before or since.

Tommy's year got off to a rousing start in March as Musselburgh hosted one of the growing number of well-financed professional tournaments, with a purse for the winner of £12, twice what Tommy had ever taken home from the Open. A dozen of Scotland's best players showed up to compete, but they were no match for the champion. Tommy romped to victory by six shots over Jamie Anderson, and then proceeded to rub his prowess in the face of Musselburgh fans who had spent a lifetime booing him and his father.

Tommy and Davie were pitted in a foursome against the Honest Toun's favourite sons, Willie Park and Bob Ferguson. The St Andrews men won all three rounds and closed out the hometown boys early. Tommy also accepted Bob's challenge to a singles match, and rallied from behind to win, avenging a rare loss he'd suffered to Ferguson the previous year and making it a clean sweep to start the season.

Just a month later came news of an astounding invitation from Royal Liverpool in England, better known as Hoylake. The club announced that its spring meeting would include a Grand

Tournament for Professionals offering the unheard of purse of £55. Fifteen would go to the winner, the largest payout ever offered.

If that wasn't attraction enough, Royal Liverpool agreed to pay the railway fees of any professional who came to play and, on top of that, to provide golfers with dinner in the evening. The club's members had subscribed more than £100 to finance the event, an enormous sum. Professional golf had reached a new, undreamt of level, and there can be no doubting the reason. Hoylake was determined to attract the man who brought legions of fans with him, along with reporters from newspapers across Scotland and England – Young Tom Morris.

It would not be the last time that Hoylake played a pivotal role in the evolution of the royal and ancient game. In 1885, the club would launch the first Amateur Championship, and in 1902 it would inaugurate the International Matches between England and Scotland, the precursor of competitions like the Walker Cup and Ryder Cup.

Tommy was no stranger to Hoylake. He had family ties there, and it may have been the place he loved best in golf. Royal Liverpool was patronised by men who were closer to his friends in the Rose Club than they were to the gentry of The R&A. Their club wasn't as steeped in class traditions as hidebound St Andrews. Tommy had played there in 1870, as he prepared for his assault on the Belt, and again in 1871, when the nine holes originally laid out by his uncle, George, were expanded to a full 18 by his cousin, Jack, the club's golf professional.

Liverpool had received its royal patronage that year and celebrated in style with what promoters billed as the first 'International Golf Match' between teams from Scotland and England. Tommy and Bob Ferguson represented Scotland. England was represented by two club professionals, Blackheath's Bob Kirk and Westward Ho!'s Johnny Allan, Tommy's childhood friend from Prestwick. It didn't matter that Bob and Johnny were Scotsmen, born and bred. Apparently, it was enough that they now worked in England. Tommy and Bob defeated the so-called English boys easily and walked away with the stake of £5. Tommy also took first prize in a professional tournament organised for the occasion.

In late April of 1872, Young Tom and leading golfers from both nations boarded trains for Hoylake to compete in the first major professional tournament held on English soil. Royal Liverpool's largesse was rewarded with an elite field of 16, a line-up as strong as any that had been assembled since Tommy's breakthrough victory at Carnoustie five years earlier. Unfortunately, Hoylake wasn't as lucky with the weather. The tournament took place on Tuesday 25 April, a bleak, rainy day with downpours so intense that play had to be suspended at times. Golfers who teed off at 11.30 weren't finished until after five o'clock. That was an eternity in an age when 36 holes routinely took less time than a modern foursome needs to finish a single round.

The competition consisted of two trips around a long, narrow, difficult course known for its wickedly fast greens. The links stretched out in front of the old Royal Hotel, which backed up to the Irish Sea. In the middle of the course was a racetrack for horses. Golf writer Bernard Darwin described it as 'a place of rather dull and mean appearance. There is none of your smug smoothness and trimness about Hoylake. It is rather hard and bare and bumpy and needs a man to conquer it.'

At the outset, it did not appear that Tommy would be all-conquering that day. He made an eight on the second hole, after landing one shot in a ditch and sending another sailing out of bounds. He finished the outward nine in a disastrous 48. Only a miracle could save his round. Tommy promptly provided it on the home nine, racing through those holes in an astonishing 37 strokes, one of the best performances of his life. At the end of the first 18, Davie Strath led the pack at 82. Tommy and Bob Andrews of Perth trailed by three strokes. Poor Bob Kirk was already all but out of the tournament. He knocked three balls off the course on Royal Liverpool's narrow first, making a 17 that led to an ugly 97.

In the second round, fighting a brutal course and grim weather, Tommy came in with the same 82 that Davie had posted on his first trip around Hoylake. It gave Tommy a total of 167 for the tournament and left Davie with another chance to show why he was the champion's most feared rival. If he could repeat the form he'd showed to start the morning, Davie would take home more money than any golfer had ever won. He couldn't quite manage it. On the last green, Davie faced a makeable putt to tie with Tommy and force a play-off. It didn't drop and Tommy added another £15 to the dozen he'd banked in March at Musselburgh.

It is hard to know what would have been more satisfying for Tommy, remaining all but invincible or enjoying Royal Liverpool's generosity. Before Tommy's meteoric rise to fame, no professional golfer would have dreamt that a gentlemen's club would pay his travel expenses and buy him dinner. Toast after toast would no doubt have been raised to Tommy, who had made this payday possible. The next morning, he and his fellow professionals boarded the train back to St Andrews, where, at last, there would be progress on the future of the tournament that had made Tommy the world's most celebrated golfer, the still dormant Open Championship.

In May, at the spring meeting of The R&A, a letter from the Prestwick secretary Harry Hart was read, laying out the proposal made the previous April that The R&A and The Honourable Company join Prestwick in buying a new Open Championship trophy. Prestwick had also proposed that the venue for the Championship rotate among the three most famous Scottish links: St Andrews, Musselburgh and Prestwick. The R&A

Green Committee was authorised to contribute up to £15 for the new trophy and to negotiate the future organisation of the Championship with the other two clubs, a process that would take all summer.

In the meantime there was plenty to occupy Tommy and fill his purse during a season he and his fellow professionals spent enjoying the fruits of his fame. Tommy still lived with his parents at 6 Pilmour Links, where the Belt was so proudly displayed. He and his father spent many days golfing together, as partners in challenge matches, or in foursomes with members of The R&A. 'Their comradeship was delightful and charming,' wrote biographer Tulloch. 'The father was proud of his son, and the son was full of affection and reverence for the father.'

Tulloch witnessed many of Tommy's matches, or was out playing his own while the young champion raked in the pounds. His biography of Old Tom records a selection of money matches that July and August involving professionals and gentlemen from The R&A. It provides a snapshot of what Tommy's life was like between trips to compete in professional tournaments and matches at the spring and autumn meetings of prominent clubs. He spent his days rubbing shoulders with wealthy and privileged men, just as he had at Ayr Academy. One afternoon he played in a foursome against Sir Alexander Kinloch, who would become captain of The R&A that year. On another he was paired with John Whyte-Melville, the club's most revered member. If gentlemen resented having to pay Tommy's price to land him as a partner – and at some level they must have – it wasn't hurting business.

Tulloch recorded 14 matches involving Young Tom that summer, which shows just how busy he was playing golf. Every season, on average, Tommy played in eight professional events. If he also played nearly twice a week with gentlemen, that means he competed for money some four dozen times a year, a schedule to rival that of any modern professional golfer. Of Tulloch's 14 matches, Tommy won nine and lost five. Two of his five losses came when he was giving competitors strokes. Two others came against teams anchored by Davie Strath.

By then Davie had earned a reputation as the only player who could give Tommy a fair fight. Davie had beaten his gifted young friend in tournaments, singles and foursomes. He'd also upstaged Tommy by being the first to win the gold medal awarded by the Rose Club. Davie only beat Tommy once in every three tries, but he always made the champion work for his money and no other golfer did nearly as well.

Davie was also Tommy's most formidable foursomes partner. Tommy was vulnerable when playing with his father, who had his shop, his greenkeeping and his course design projects to distract him. But Tommy and Davie were well-nigh invincible. Looking back on his storied career, Bob Ferguson would remember the day he and Willie Park vanquished Tommy and Davie at North Berwick as one of his finest moments.

Just as Willie had before them, Tommy and Davie brazenly published challenges in national newspapers offering to take on any comers for any sum, alone or as a team. If no one stepped up – and why would they? – Tommy and Davie played against each other in singles or foursomes. The Rose Club was behind it all. Summertime matches that the club staged featuring its leading lights became The Greatest Show in Golf, enthralling vacationers who often were seeing the game played for the first time. It only piqued interest that Tommy and Davie were glamour boys inclined to live lavishly. Every match between them was hyped by the press, sent gamblers scrambling to the bookmaker, and drew thousands of fans to the golf course.

That was the case on 24 August, when Tommy and Davie played on opposite sides of a foursome that proved to be the highlight of the summer of 1872. Tommy and his father took on Davie and Tom Kidd, a young St Andrews professional who was on the verge of making his mark in the game. Sturdy and square-jawed, sporting fashionable togs, mutton chops and a moustache, Kidd was a phenomenally long driver. His Herculean tee shots sailed past those of every player he faced, Tommy included. Kidd had come up the hard way, emerging from the ranks of caddies to become one of the game's most promising players. Like so many St Andrews men, he was from a family of weavers who had to find new jobs when industrialisation made hand looms obsolete. Carrying clubs turned out to be Kidd's best option.

Betting on the contest was intense, as usual. Tommy and his father opened as the 5/4 favourites. That was no surprise, given how long they had been the marquee pairing. But ever since he left his clerk's job four years ago, Davie had been playing a formidable game, and now he was paired with a bomber. By the time the four of them gathered on the first tee, Davie and Kidd had picked up so much support that the odds were even. Excitement over the 36-hole match reached such a pitch that the English magazine *The Field* sent a correspondent to record every shot. Tulloch reprinted the clipping in his biography as an example of the expansive coverage professional golf was receiving in national newspapers and magazines.

It had been a miserable summer in St Andrews, but the weather was finally starting to turn on the morning the match began. That Saturday dawned dull and cloudy, tempering the withering heat that had suffocated the town for weeks. Nevertheless, the links remained in prime condition, except for a few places where the grass had grown unmanageably thick. At 11.30, Old Tom belted the first shot towards the Swilcan Burn in front of an electric crowd that followed the foursome around the course.

In round one, the teams were like prizefighters trading blows. The lead changed hands twice before the players finished the front nine, and it would be that way all afternoon. Every time

Davie and Kidd landed a punch, the Morrises bounced off the ropes to square the match. Both sides had taken and lost the lead twice more on the back nine before Tommy and his father went one up at 15 with the holes dwindling down. Their only reward was to see Davie land a haymaker. On the 16th, Kidd knocked their team's ball far off line into a hollow. From there, Davie played a gorgeous cleek shot to halve the hole and prevent his side from falling hopelessly behind. It was the kind of shot that ignites a team. Davie and Kidd went on to win 17 and 18 and nip their foes one up in the first round.

That only ratcheted up interest in the second and deciding round of the match. Early on, however, it became clear that fortune favoured the square-jawed caddie and his elegant partner. Kidd holed a long putt on the first green to give his team a two-up lead. On the second, he laid the Morrises a stymie, placing his ball directly between theirs and the cup. Daring as ever, Tommy tried to putt around it, but instead his ball hit Kidd's and knocked it in. Davie and Kidd won the hole. Suddenly, father and son were three down. But the Morrises were not inclined to panic. They had faced this kind of crisis many times, and as always they fought back bravely, with Tommy leading the way by holing spectacular putts.

By the time the foursome reached the 16th tee, the Morrises had cut the lead to one. Three holes remained for them to overtake Davie and Kidd, including the dangerous 17th. That was plenty of time for players of their calibre and experience. Gamblers who had the nerve to bet against Tommy and his father had to feel queasy, but Davie and Kidd calmly delivered the knockout punch. They won the 16th to go dormy, two up with two to play. On the famed Road Hole, it was Tommy and his father who were ensnared. Their approach to the green landed in its treacherous bunker, and the match was over. It was a landmark victory for Davie, cementing his reputation as

Tommy's most dangerous opponent and priming the pump for even more stirring battles to come.

Three weeks after that match came the news everyone in golf had been anticipating for nearly a year now. The Open Championship was about to be resumed. Prestwick, The Royal and Ancient and The Honourable Company had each agreed to chip in £10 in order to acquire a new Golf Champion's trophy, a silver claret jug made by Mackay, Cunningham & Company of Edinburgh. It was nearly identical to the prize that had been offered in 1857, when gentlemen golfers competed in Colonel Fairlie's first Grand National Tournament at St Andrews.

For this new Open, however, the rules would be different to when the Championship started. No golfer would get to keep the Claret Jug, no matter how many times he won the Open. It would have to be returned the following year. The trophy wasn't finished in time for the 1872 Championship, so the clubs decided to give the winner a gold medal. That tradition continues to this day, with the secretary of The R&A intoning solemnly at every prize ceremony, 'And now, the winner of the gold medal and the Champion Golfer of the Year.'

The three clubs finalised their agreement to resume the Open at the absolute last minute. It was signed on 11 September 1872 – two days before the first of the new Championships was to be contested at Prestwick, its original home. St Andrews and Musselburgh would follow in the newly established rota. Perhaps not surprisingly, just eight players assembled in Ayrshire for that Open, the smallest field since Old Tom's record win by 13 strokes a decade earlier.

Who knows if the paltry turnout was the result of a last-minute decision, a winner's share that was just £8 when £15 was offered elsewhere, or the dominance Tommy had displayed in professional tournaments that season at Musselburgh and Hoylake. Whatever the reason, there was no Willie Park, no Bob

Andrews and no Bob Kirk. What mattered to the fans, however, was that the Open featured the two debonair dandies of golf, Tommy and Davie. Old Tom, David Park of Musselburgh fame and the talented amateur William Doleman were also along for the ride.

That was good enough for *The Field*, whose correspondent opened his report with an enthusiastic declaration that the Open had been saved: 'It will thus be observed that the champions' competition is now thoroughly established, which will tend to increase the popularity of this elegant and healthy pastime.' That would turn out to be true, as a record 26 players gathered for the first Championship at St Andrews the following year and, with few exceptions, the size of the field grew steadily after that.

As always, a tremendous crowd turned up at Prestwick for the tournament. It was played on 13 September, just as the Ayrshire coast was emerging from a stretch of dreary, rainy days. The weather was pleasant that Friday morning, crisp and clear, although a stiff breeze blowing from the west made it a tough day for scoring. It didn't help that the greens were soft and shaggy from storms that had pelted the course all week.

Tommy, naturally, was the overwhelming favourite, and as reigning champion led the field off the first tee. He played mediocre golf in the opening rounds, missing one short putt after another on those soggy greens, shades of his father. His one moment of glory came at The Wall, the hole that had so often been his undoing. Tommy's approach shot sailed long, landing three inches from an old stone wall that ran behind the green. What to do? As always Tommy opted for the riskiest shot. He tried to knock the ball against the dyke with an iron and have it ricochet back onto the green. Instead it climbed over the wall and into no man's land beyond. Tommy calmly jumped the wall with his club in hand, and, with the hole completely out of view, landed one close and then knocked it in.

Aside from that spectacular shot – which ranks with the most memorable of Tommy's career – there was not a lot for his backers to cheer about after the first two rounds had been completed. Tommy finished round one in 57, worse than any score he had made during his run for the Belt. He found himself a stroke behind Davie. Strath turned it on in the second round, coming in with a 52 as Tommy made another pedestrian 56. Now Davie was sitting on a five-stroke lead with just 12 holes left, poised to win his first Open. Gamblers who roamed the fairways offering bettors new odds as the tide turned apparently were convinced that Davie had the upper hand. 'Young Tom, the champion, was the favourite until the commencement of the third round, when Strath started with five strokes of advantage,' *The Field* reported. 'The betting consequently went in his favour, 5/4 being offered.'

That must have annoyed Tommy, because he turned up the heat, especially where his game could be most devastating, on the green. 'His putting, although not always successful, has hitherto not been surpassed on these links,' the magazine concluded. That is saying something considering the way Young Tom had putted in the past at Prestwick. He came in with 53 for a final score of 166 – nearly a dozen strokes higher than any score he had posted in his three victories to retire the Belt.

Always prone to nerves, Davie succumbed to them in the final round. His troubles began on the second hole, the famed Alps, considered then and now to be one of the most intimidating in golf. The player approaching that green stands in a deep valley staring up at a mammoth dune, beyond which the hole lies unseen. Davie hit what *The Field* charitably described as 'an unfortunate iron shot'. It cost him three strokes. On the last hole, when all must have seemed lost, he knocked his ball into the Goosedubs swamp. The upshot? Davie scored 61 on his third trip around Prestwick and finished second by three strokes as Tommy added another £8 to his bankroll.

For the fourth consecutive time – a record then and now – Young Tom was Scotland's Champion Golfer. The next day he and his father finished Prestwick's autumn meeting in style by beating Davie and David Park in a foursome by a single hole.

Six weeks later, at Royal Aberdeen in north-east Scotland, Tommy's dream season came to its rightful conclusion. He lapped a field of a dozen professionals in the last big-money event of 1872, a tournament that paid the winner £15, matching Hoylake's extravagance. Tommy traded blows with Davie in the first trip around the 14-hole course. Both players came in with 60, just a shade over level fours. But, as he so often did, Tommy ran away from Davie and the pack in the final round with a 58. Davie still took second, but he limped in a full ten strokes behind the winner.

What an astonishing season it had been. Tommy had played in five tournaments and won four of them. He had prevailed in both of his high-stakes singles matches and three of his four foursomes. He'd won a staggering 80 per cent of his events. Tommy had failed to take top honours only when Bob Martin, a workman in Old Tom's shop, won the professional tournament at St Andrews that autumn and when Davie and Tom Kidd defeated him and his father in that celebrated summertime foursome. In all of golf history, rare is the season that can compare to what Tommy accomplished in 1872. His winnings for the year tell the tale. They amounted to £200, four times his father's annual salary. There could no longer be any question about whether a man could make a decent living simply by playing golf. Young Tom had become fabulously well-to-do for a man born to the working class.

In the aftermath of that glorious year, it is worth reflecting on what historian Everard wrote about the failure of Scotland's leading clubs to pull together and host an Open Championship in 1871. It was, indeed, tough luck for the young champion, because if 1872 proved anything it was that Tommy's game was so all-powerful in those years that it is doubtful any player could have wrested his crown. What a feat it would have been – and in hindsight how inevitable it seems – for Tommy to have won five Championships in succession.

When Young Tommy made his golfing debut at Perth as a mere boy of twelve, he was invited to pose with the assembled professionals for a photograph taken to commemorate the event. That spoke volumes about the respect he had already earned as a player. Even then the fierce intensity that would be the hallmark of Tommy's professional career was evident in his eyes. *From a private collection.*

The professionals who competed in the Perth Open of 1864 were not wild about the idea of a 12-year-old boy playing in the tournament. That is one of the reasons Young Tommy's exploits in the Fair City were confined to a singles match against the town's best young player, William Greig. Tommy's dominant victory was witnessed by a crowd far larger than the one that had seen his father win the Perth Open over a field that included such stars as Willie and David Park, William Dow, and local hero Bob Andrews. *From a private collection.*

Young Tommy's prowess on the links was perhaps the best advertisement for his father's club-and-ball making shop in the heart of St Andrews. This image, made when Tommy was in his teens, is from a trade card ordered by his father. Like any doting parent, Tom loved nothing more than entertaining visitors to his shop with tales of his famous son. *From a private collection.*

The full trading card featured both Tommy and his brother Jof and commemorated their record-tying rounds of 77 over the links of St Andrews. *From a private collection.*

Young Tom's trips south of the border captured the imagination of golfers there and helped ignite the great English golf boom. Within five years after Tommy's death, golf was spreading like wildfire in England. This image is a detail from a group photo taken at Royal North Devon in 1870 as Tommy prepared to claim the Belt. *Courtesy of the Royal North Devon Golf Club*

The iconic image of Young Tommy shows him wearing The Champion's Belt shortly after his overpowering victory in 1870 secured that glittering prize as his personal property. Just nineteen years old, Tommy dresses like a dandy, with piping on his jacket, pin-striped slacks, a lush silk tie, and a gold watch chain draped across his waistcoat. But for a wisp of a mustache he is fresh-faced, a style favored by young lovers of the Victorian age. *Courtesy of the University of St Andrews Library*

Tom Morris + Tommy Morris

T. RODGER   S^T ANDREWS

In 1875 Tommy and his father posed for this portrait in the studio of his friend Thomas Rodger. Now married to Margaret Drinnen and expecting a child, Tommy favours manly-looking mutton chops to complement his mustache. He and his father spent that summer preparing for a celebrated match of Open Champions that autumn at North Berwick against Willie and Mungo Park of Musselburgh. *From a private collection.*

Young Tommy's final match was played in bitter winter weather in St Andrews against Arthur Molesworth, a famed amateur from Westward Ho! It spanned 216 holes and Tommy won easily despite allowing Arthur six strokes every round. The final eighteen holes were played in a snowstorm. That inspired this painting by Major F. P. Hopkins, a well-known golf artist, which depicts Tommy trying to pitch the ball over the snow to an area around the hole that has been swept clear for putting. *Reproduced by kind permission of the Royal and Ancient Golf Club of St Andrews*

Tommy's best friend and fiercest rival, Davie Strath, had much in common with Scotland's undisputed Champion Golfer. Like Tommy, Davie was an educated man. He worked in a lawyer's office and was considered the only golfer of the age who could give Tommy a run for his money. Their matches proved to be a turning point in the history of the game. *From a private collection.*

Anderson

Jamie Anderson, son of a celebrated St Andrews character, would rank with the greatest players of Tommy's age. He beat Tommy to the punch in setting the record of 77 at St Andrews and became the first player after the young champion to win three Opens in succession. His style was not marked by dash or vigor, like Tommy's, but by what a contemporary described as 'a dead level of steadiness'. *From a private collection.*

For St Andrews men the most heated rivalries were with players from Musselburgh, the city's only challenger as capital of the Scottish game. Tommy's Musselburgh foe was Bob Ferguson. Bob also arrived on the scene in 1867, winning a tournament at Leith. He seldom got the best of Tommy, but always made the young superstar fight for his victories. Bob also went on to win three consecutive Opens and nearly four, narrowly losing a heartbreaking playoff in 1883.

The feisty Bob Kirk, pictured here with Tommy, was one of the few players of his age to defeat the young champion in a singles match. He never finished better than second in the Open Championship, managing that three times, but he was a formidable foursome partner, especially when paired with Old Tom. *From a private collection.*

Photo by J. Hardie.

BOB KIRK.   **YOUNG TOM MORRIS.**

Tommy's first days on the links were spent with his childhood friend, James Hunter, whose parents were the proprietors of the Red Lion Inn, the original home of the Prestwick Golf Club. *From a private collection.*

Young Tommy's sister Lizzie, with whom he posed for this portrait in 1868, married one of her brother's childhood friends, James Hunter. James became a wealthy timber merchant in America, securing the financial future of the already well-established Morris family. Following her mother's death in 1876, Lizzie moved back to the family home in St Andrews to care for her father and brothers for the remainder of her days. *From a private collection.*

Jof Morris was never a match for his older brother, although he was an accomplished golfer who once finished third in the Open Championship and equalled Tommy's 77 over the links of St Andrews. *From a private collection.*

In 1864, after 14 years at Prestwick, Tom Morris was persuaded to return to St Andrews and care for its famed links. He and his family moved from Prestwick back to his home town, the old grey city by the sea. There, over the next four decades, Tom would emerge as the Grand Old Man of golf and perhaps the most influential figure in the history of the royal and ancient game. *From a private collection.*

By 1895, a generation after his famous son's death, Old Tom had become the most revered figure in the game. *From a private collection.*

Before the ascent of Young Tommy, Scotland's undisputed champion golfer was Allan Robertson. The jovial, mutton-chopped feather ball maker set the course record of 79 for the links at St Andrews. He also teamed up with Old Tom Morris, to win the most storied foursome match in early golf history over the Dunn brothers of Musselburgh. *From a private collection.*

The anti-hero of Tommy's childhood, the brash Willie Park of Musselburgh, dashed the hopes of Prestwick fans when he won the first Open Championship in 1860, with Old Tom runner up. This portrait of Willie, wearing his signature bow tie, was taken that same year. *From a private collection.*

Colonel James Ogilvy Fairlie, a man of unflappable temperament and bold ideas, became Tom Morris's partner and mentor in golf. In 1851, he lured Tom to Prestwick to lay out a proper links there. Prestwick would create the first national competition for professional golfers, the tournament that evolved into the Open Championship. A fine golfer and all-around sportsman, Fairlie poses here over a shot as Tom stands behind carrying his clubs. Also pictured are three of Fairlie's sons, Sir Hope Grant, and his caddie. *From a private collection.*

The Challenge Belt, the original trophy for the Open Championship, was a twenty-five pound jewel crafted of red moroccan leather with a gleaming silver buckle engraved with a golfing scene. After Tommy claimed The Belt as his personal property – by winning it three times in succession as proscribed by the rules -- it became popularly known as The Champion's Belt. In 1908, following the death of Old Tom Morris, his descendants donated their grandfather's prized possession to the Royal and Ancient Golf Club of St Andrews. *Courtesy of the University of St Andrews Library*

IN MEMORY OF
"TOMMY"
SON OF THOMAS MORRIS
WHO DIED 25ᵀᴴ DECEMBER 1875 AGED 24 YEARS

DEEPLY REGRETTED BY NUMEROUS FRIENDS AND ALL GOLFERS
HE THRICE IN SUCCESSION WON THE CHAMPION'S BELT
AND HELD IT WITHOUT RIVALRY AND YET WITHOUT ENVY
HIS MANY AMIABLE QUALITIES
BEING NO LESS ACKNOWLEDGED THAN HIS GOLFING ACHIEVEMENTS

THIS MONUMENT HAS BEEN ERECTED
BY CONTRIBUTIONS FROM SIXTY GOLFING SOCIETIES

In 1878, three years after Tommy's death at age twenty-four plunged St Andrews into mourning this memorial to Scotland's once-and-forever King of Clubs was unveiled in the cathedral burial ground. Built with contributions from all sixty leading golf clubs of the age, it rise to the height of the stone wall surrounding that ancient burial ground and towers over every gravestone in a cemetery where luminaries have been buried for centuries.

Ten

MATCH PLAY

———— •●◉●• ————

Since he was a young boy in Prestwick, taking his first swings with a club made in his father's shop, golf had been Tommy's all-consuming passion. That changed in 1873, the year he fell in love with a dark-haired beauty who had a forbidden past.

Her name was Margaret Drinnen. She was a coal miner's daughter from the industrial heartland of Scotland, a region between Edinburgh and Glasgow known as West Lothian. For the past two years, she had been working as a housemaid for a couple who lived in a fashionable neighbourhood adjacent to the St Andrews Links. Landing that job had been Margaret's salvation.

Eight years earlier, in the summer of 1866, she had suffered the indignity of standing before her parish, her family and her friends to be admonished for the sin of fornication. That spring, at the age of 25, Margaret had borne a daughter out of wedlock, ordinarily a ruinous event for a woman growing up in Victorian Scotland. She had no choice but to endure the public humiliation known as naming and shaming if she wanted to have young

Helen baptised at her parish church in nearby Whitburn. The baptism was urgently needed, as the baby died two weeks later.

The church elders took pity on Margaret. She got a slap on the wrist and her daughter was baptised that same day. Margaret's elder sister, also named Helen after their mother, hadn't been let off nearly as easily when she was shamed three years earlier. She was severely rebuked and forced to come back the following Sunday for an examination on the meaning of baptism before her child was welcomed into the fold.

The parish elders may simply have felt sorry for Margaret because her baby was deathly ill. She may also have been charming enough, while admitting her sin, to earn her reprieve. Tall, dark-haired, with striking features, Margaret was by all accounts a captivating woman. The Reverend A.K.H. Boyd, who came to know her as the spiritual leader of Holy Trinity in St Andrews, remembered her in his memoir as 'a remarkably handsome and healthy young woman: most lovable in every way'. He appears not to have known that Margaret had given birth to a child before she was married. If he did, he was too gentlemanly to mention it.

Margaret was one of six children born to Walter and Helen Drinnen. They lived in Crofthead, a desperate assemblage of two-room cottages slapped together for workers by the Coltness Iron Company. Margaret's father worked there digging seams from which coal and ironstone were mined. When she was nine years old, Margaret began an apprenticeship doing fine needlework on garments to give them individuality and flair. Years later she made the step up to housemaid, a coveted position because it meant living in a beautiful home and being well clothed and fed. She thrived in that job, eventually being referred to the couple in St Andrews.

Margaret moved to the 'city by the sea' sometime after the census was taken in April of 1871. It was the fresh start she needed. St Andrews must have seemed like heaven to a woman who had grown up in the sulphurous grime of coal country. No one knows how or where Tommy met Margaret. She can't have been in St Andrews long before she began hearing stories about the flamboyant Champion Golfer and dashing leader of the Rose Club and its cadre of bright, aspiring young men.

She and Tommy may have met on any number of occasions. They may have crossed paths at a Sunday service or church supper. Every God-fearing Presbyterian attended Holy Trinity on Sundays, and the most steadfast among them, Old Tom, kept the links closed on the Sabbath. They may have met at one of the balls held regularly in town, or one of the dance classes men and women attended to prepare for those social occasions so important to Victorian courtship.

Margaret would seem the most unexpected of choices for Tommy. She came from a vastly different world, a class level considered far below his, and she was ten years older than him. Perhaps Tommy was simply swept away by her beauty. Perhaps he saw in Margaret, who had overcome so many obstacles in life, something of his own fighting spirit. Or perhaps he was drawn to her simply because she was older. Tommy had been in the spotlight since he was 12 years old, spending much of that time with older men. Boys in that situation grow up quickly. He may simply have preferred a mate who was more mature than women his own age. Whatever attracted Tommy to Margaret, in courting her he did what he had been doing all his life. He made his own choice and convention be damned.

It is, perhaps, less difficult to understand why Margaret became smitten with Tommy. Their courtship began developing at a time when he was the centre of attention in St Andrews, the summer of 1873. That was the year Jules Verne captured the imagination of readers with *Around the World in 80 Days*, his novel about Phileas Fogg's circumnavigation of the globe by train and steamship. It was the year that Susan B. Anthony was arrested for voting in the US presidential election, a seminal moment for suffragettes. It was also the year that Tommy and Davie Strath played their first Great Matches, two marathons as hyped for the Victorian era as the Ali–Frazier boxing extravaganzas would be in another age. Both the *Daily News* and *Times of London* sent correspondents to wire daily dispatches from St Andrews. Even the *Ladies' Home Journal* felt compelled to keep its genteel readers up to date on 'the madness' surrounding 'The Great St Andrews Golf Match'.

It was amid this whirlwind that Tommy and Margaret met and fell in love. One can hardly imagine how she felt about that turn of events. On that long-ago afternoon when she stood before her congregation to be shamed, her future must have seemed hopeless. Now she had captured the heart of a man whose every step on the links was followed by adoring crowds, a man who won more money than a woman who grew up in West Lothian could dream of earning. Busy as Margaret would have been with her work as a maid, she surely would have tried to catch some of the action as her new beau and Davie staged their heroic battles over the St Andrews Links, just a brisk walk down the street. Everyone in town was doing the same thing.

The timing of these matches was impeccable. For six years, Tommy had towered over the game, but now his suave rival seemed to be closing in. Davie had beaten Tommy in the final tournament of 1871 at Carnoustie, and the following year he and Tom Kidd had taken Tommy and his father down in that ballyhooed foursome at St Andrews. The clincher turned out to be a pair of 36-hole matches which Tommy and Davie played at The R&A's spring meeting in 1873. Critically, Davie won the first match by two holes. When Tommy took the rematch by the same score, gamblers knew their moment had arrived. Before a month had passed, the first Great Match between Tommy and Davie had been arranged for £100 a side. It would span three days of 36 holes each over the links, and would be all anyone talked about that summer in St Andrews and the world of golf beyond.

Tommy and Davie presented a study in contrasts as golfers, slashing bravado versus smooth elegance. They had been battling one another since they were teenagers. Now both were in their prime. Tommy was 22, Davie 24. Money aside, there can't be any doubt that both men desperately wanted to win the match. Davie's reputation, especially, rode on the outcome. Nothing could overshadow what Tommy had accomplished already, but losing on his home turf would take even him down a peg.

Both men had fellow professionals as caddies for the most important battle of their lives. Jamie Anderson carried Tommy's clubs. Steady and reliable, he was just the man a fearless player like Tommy needed whispering in his ear during a big match. Tom Kidd accompanied Davie. Perhaps he thought having the long-driving caddie by his side would bring him luck after their victory the previous summer.

The first Great Match was played over the last week of July in typical Scottish weather, as wind and rain alternated with blue skies and summer sun. Thousands of fans swarmed the links to follow the gallant superstars, while countless others across Scotland and England read about every shot in breathless reports by the sporting press. Newspapers made a point of noting what a tough job the umpire for the match, R&A stalwart Major Robert Boothby, faced in corralling the unruly herd that lined the fairways. No doubt that was partly because fans had more than the competition to get their hearts pumping. Betting on the Great Match was extraordinary, in both England and Scotland, even for a sport that had always been as much about wagering as golf. It is a safe bet that few among the throng following the action had missed the chance to risk part of the monthly rent on their man.

Tommy and Davie waged a pitched battle from the outset, characterised by spectacular shots and phenomenally low scoring.

Neither player could get more than two holes ahead in the early going. After two trips around the links, the first day of the match ended in a tie. Day two started the same way. Tommy and Davie fought to a draw on the first 18 holes before settling in for the lunch break. That afternoon, however, Davie played the most inspired golf of his life. He drove the ball brilliantly, sailing past Tommy's tee shot on many holes, and putted even better. Davie's marvellous score of 81, just four strokes off the course record, gave him an imposing four-hole lead as the second day of the Great Match drew to a close. His backers – and there were more of them now than ever – had to be palpitating in anticipation of the final two rounds the next morning.

Tommy, of course, was never one to be counted out, no matter how far behind he might fall. Bob Ferguson could attest to that. He had watched the young champion rally from three holes down with just nine to play and crush his hopes on the final green. Tommy was at his invincible best over the first 18 the next morning, knocking in putts from everywhere and coming in with 84 on his way to winning back all four holes. Suddenly, the Great Match was all square again with just 18 to play.

Those who had risked their money on Davie no doubt feared he was wilting again under Tommy's relentless assault. They had to be even more worried when he found himself two holes down as the players approached the tenth tee in the final round. Davie wasted no time calming those fears. He stormed through the opening holes of the back nine to take a three-up lead with just four holes remaining. Even Tommy couldn't close that gap. Davie finished him off on the 16th green, winning the Great Match by three up with two to play. Victory would never be sweeter for Davie. He must have reaped generous rewards from gentlemen who had made a fortune betting on him.

The inevitable rematch was arranged within days. The stake would be smaller this time, £50 a side, but it would be another heroic, three-day battle of 108 holes. It took place over the St Andrews Links during the last week of August. By then, interest in Tommy and Davie had reached boiling point 'in all parts of the kingdom', as *The Field* put it. That was evident from the extravagant amount of money bet on the outcome, which surpassed even the heavy wagering on Tommy and Davie's match the previous month. Newspapers reported the total as £2,000, a staggering sum that was enough to keep 50 Scottish families housed and fed for a year. Nearly a third of that amount was bet in Liverpool alone, attesting to the duo's drawing power in England. Odds were even at the outset. But before the two players approached the first tee, again with Jamie and Kidd as their caddies, Davie had emerged as the slight favourite. One can imagine how the 'Goliath of his generation' felt about that.

The weather was worse for this encounter than it had been for their first match in July. Steady rain often pelted the course as the players made their way around the links. That didn't faze fans. The crowds that jammed the fairways for the second act of this drama were even larger than those that had assembled four weeks earlier. This time their numbers included famous golfers from across Scotland. Intense press coverage had spread the word to every place where the game was played that something historic was unfolding at St Andrews. No golfer worthy of the name wanted to miss that.

On the first day of the match, Davie came out playing even more brilliantly than he had in July. He raced out to another daunting lead over the first 36 holes, finishing four up. Tommy's situation became even more dire when the battle resumed the following morning. Again Davie won the opening round, this time by a single hole. He needed just 39 strokes on the back nine, a spectacular score. As he walked off the course for the lunch break, Davie must have felt supremely confident. His lead now stood at an imposing five holes. His backers were probably counting their winnings.

Tommy, however, still had 18 holes to play that day and another 36 the following afternoon. He wasn't about to be beaten twice in a row by any man alive. 'With characteristic and indomitable determination,' Tulloch wrote, 'Tommy concentrated his energies for a desperate fight.'

In those final three rounds, Davie must have learned how Bob Ferguson felt on that memorable day at Luffness when Tommy seemed always to be striding confidently towards the next tee with the words, 'Pick it out of the hole, laddie.' Tommy dropped bombs from all over St Andrews' massive, undulating greens. He came in with scores of 82, 83 and 85, astonishing consistency in such a crucible of pressure. Tommy's prowess clearly rattled Davie, who had often lamented that if he could putt like Tommy he would fear no man. Davie went around the final 18 in 90, the worst score either player turned in during the Great Match. He didn't win a single hole. Tommy wiped out Davie's five-up lead and went on to win by four holes. It was a crucial victory. With Davie having taken the opener convincingly and become the betting favourite for the rematch, Tommy needed to show the world that he was still Scotland's King of Clubs. He'd done just that, in style.

The Great Matches of 1873 will be remembered as the moment when golf stopped being a mere Scottish pastime and took its place among Britain's popular spectator sports. It had been a generation since the introduction of the gutty ball began attracting droves of new fans to the game. During those years, Tommy had achieved a pinnacle of fame unmatched in his sport. It proved to be a transformative combination – again, in part, because of exquisite timing. The matches between Tommy and Davie were played just as sports were becoming an important aspect of Victorian cultural life. Victorians believed that playing cricket, football, rugby or golf instilled such values as character, teamwork and responsibility and helped bridge the gap between people of different classes. Amid this burgeoning interest in games, Tommy and Davie's matches captured the imagination of the masses, especially sportsmen in England, in a way no golf spectacle ever had. The lavish press coverage their matches received and the massive wagering on the outcome prove that beyond doubt. Not even The Great Foursome of 1849 or the disputed grudge match between Old Tom and Willie Park in 1870 had aroused such widespread and rabid interest. From that moment forward, the royal and ancient game was assured of its place on sports pages and its share of passionate devotees.

Tommy and Davie's matches that summer would also be remembered as the finest display of golf the game had seen in its first four centuries. They were played at a time when only Allan, Old Tom, Jamie and Tommy had broken 80 at St Andrews. Winning scores in the annual professional tournament there typically were half a dozen strokes higher. Viewed in that context, Tommy and Davie's scores over the 12 rounds boggle the mind. Both players turned in five rounds of 84 or less. Davie raced through nine holes in 39 not once but twice, a feat that had been achieved fewer than six times at St Andrews. Tommy finished nine holes in 40 three times and had a dozen nines of 42 or less. After 12 gruelling rounds, just a single hole separated the two golfers. Even more remarkably, they took precisely the same number of strokes – 1,027 each, an average of 85.5 per round.

Nearly two decades later, the historian Everard sized up The Great Matches of 1873 in an essay for Badminton Library's *Golf*. By that time, Everard had seen both Jamie Anderson and Bob Ferguson win three consecutive Opens, Bob nearly four. He had seen the rise of the great British golfers John Henry Taylor, Harry Vardon and John Ball, the first amateur to win an Open. And yet, he had this to say about those monumental battles between Tommy and Davie: 'For brilliant and steady play combined with the absence of mistakes, the golf that these two exhibited has never been surpassed.'

In the afterglow of that summer, the 'Tommy and Davie Show' moved north to Aberdeen, one of many cities putting up cash to attract the game's brightest stars. Their match for £15 provided entertainment for Prince Leopold, a distinguished visitor who would soon become captain of The Royal and Ancient Golf Club. Tommy won again, going four holes up with two to play. He was winning as regularly as ever, becoming richer by the day, but golf was hardly the only matter on Tommy's mind. His courtship of Margaret was by this time taking a serious turn.

In Victorian Scotland, even for a member of the working class, courtship was a slow, careful business. It was viewed not simply as a romance but as a career move, given that any property a woman possessed or any dowry her family offered reverted to the man after marriage. Once they had been properly introduced – single women never approached a man without an introduction – they would spend time walking together, perhaps strolling along the seaside or among the ruins in the cathedral churchyard. They would always have a chaperone along, usually an older family member and preferably someone who was married.

If their walks sparked a mutual attraction, they would begin keeping company regularly. But until a couple was engaged there could be no sexual contact. No holding hands, no kissing, and absolutely no being left alone together in a room or carriage. Once an engagement had been announced, the rules loosened up a bit. Couples were permitted to walk or take a carriage by themselves, to hold hands in public, and perhaps to steal a chaste kiss. It is hard to know, of course, how closely a nonconformist like Tommy would have stuck to Victorian conventions. But in this case, even he would likely have been inclined to follow the rules to make life easier in town for the woman who would become his wife.

The intensity of Tommy's focus on courting Margaret was, perhaps, evident in the way he played during the waning months of 1873 and early the next spring. He showed little of the fierce intensity he had displayed when he bounced off the ropes to defeat Davie that summer at St Andrews and reinforced his supremacy two weeks later in the presence of a prince. It may simply have been the kind of comedown that countless athletes experience after such a peak performance. But the more likely explanation is that his mind was on winning Margaret and nothing else. Either way the 1873 Open – the first to be played at Tommy's home course – turned out to be depressing for him and his legion of fans.

St Andrews had been drenched by torrential rains in the days before a record field of 26 players assembled for the Championship on Saturday 4 October. The course was a bog, with standing water everywhere. That was a significant issue, as the rules in those days did not allow a player to remove his ball from a puddle without costing himself a one-stroke penalty. The soggy conditions negated Tommy's principal advantage. Great putting was impossible with the greens so wet. The champion hobbled in after the first round with an unimaginable 94, the highest score he had ever recorded in an Open. No doubt it included numerous penalties for removing his ball from the water that saturated the links.

Jamie Anderson, Bob Kirk and the long-hitting Kidd were tied for the lead at 91 after the first 18. Those scores weren't anything to brag about either, even over a links that presented a gruelling test of golf. Tommy fought back gamely in the second round, coming in with the second-lowest score of the Championship at 89. It was not enough. Kidd did one better with 88. The fashionably attired caddie stunned every golf fan and gamblers across Britain by becoming the unlikely player who finally wrested Tommy's crown as Champion Golfer. Jamie finished second, a stroke behind Kidd at 180. Tommy and Kirk tied for third at 183, while Davie straggled in four strokes behind them with scores of 97 and 90.

No one could have predicted Kidd's victory. His total of 179 was the highest winning score ever recorded in an Open and would remain so until the event was extended to 72 holes in 1892. He would never win another Championship, although in years to come he would prove to be a formidable foursome partner for Old Tom. The result was so shocking that the reporter who covered the Open felt obliged to explain the outcome. 'Tom Kidd, who by the result of this competition won for himself the high honour of champion, has already proved to be an excellent player and distinguished himself in many singles and foursomes, and the honour thus gained will consequently be grudged him the less, although he won it with so high a score,' the writer reasoned.

While course conditions played a significant part in Tommy's first defeat in the Open since 1867, he was also facing the consequences of his supremacy. He had raised the game to a new level. Like every transcendent player who would follow him, Tommy now had to cope with men like Kidd who had risen to the challenge. Davie was playing the best golf of his life, and so were Jamie and Bob Ferguson.

Tommy also failed to reclaim his mantle as Champion Golfer in the 1874 Open, which in a curious turn of events took place just six months later. That first Championship at Musselburgh was held on 10 April, in association with the spring meeting of The Honourable Company of Edinburgh Golfers. The reasons for Tommy's second consecutive loss were much the same as his first. Heavy rain and hail pelted the course all morning. The weather had just cleared before Tommy and Willie Park led another record field of 32 players off the tee at noon, driving into a stiff breeze that blew for all four trips around that ancient nine-hole links.

A massive crowd followed Tommy and Willie, but neither was at his sparkling best. Tommy hit his drive from the second tee so far sideways that it landed on a road that ran beside the course. Both he and Willie finished the first 18 holes with scores of 83, solid but unspectacular on the far less imposing

Musselburgh links. Willie's younger brother Mungo surged out to a comfortable lead with a brilliant 75. Tommy made his charge in round two. He came in with a valiant 78, again the second-lowest score of the Championship. Still, he would fall just short. Mungo held on to win by two, despite nearly throwing away the Open with an 84 in his final round. Davie Strath played terribly, finishing last with rounds of 86 and 90.

Tommy can be forgiven if his mind was wandering. By then he had decided to take the most radical step of his life, marrying Margaret. In June of 1874, just two months after the Open, Tommy prepared for his wedding by having Reverend Boyd give him his first communion at Holy Trinity. In November, the 23-year-old superstar's impending marriage was announced from the pulpit of the church.

More than anything Tommy had ever done – more than setting his own terms in foursomes with gentlemen, more than impertinently behaving as if he were equal to the lords of The R&A – marrying Margaret demonstrated his utter disregard for the conventions that governed Victorian society. Tommy loved Margaret and that was that.

He must have known that choosing to marry a woman with her background would be scorned in staid St Andrews, creating an impossibly awkward social situation for his parents. He must have known that Old Tom and Nancy expected so much more of him. He had been educated at Scotland's premier academy. He had substantial earning power as the world's greatest golfer. His parents had every right to expect that Tommy would marry up, as his sister Lizzie would do when she married James Hunter, Tommy's childhood friend from Prestwick, who became a highly successful and respected timber merchant in America. It must have been disappointing to Old Tom and Nancy that their son's heart was won by a woman from Scotland's grim underbelly, with outwardly no prospects whatsoever.

Old Tom never wrote or spoke about the marriage, although the evidence seems overwhelming that he and Nancy disapproved. Neither he nor his wife attended the ceremony, which took place in Whitburn on 25 November 1874. It is true that Nancy was suffering with chronic rheumatism by then and was often in great pain, but one year later she and her husband both attended Lizzie's wedding. Old Tom did, at least, acknowledge the occasion, throwing a party at Honeyman's Golf Hotel on the day of the wedding for his workmen and a few friends.

Tommy's eldest brother, Jof, did not serve as best man at the wedding, as tradition would dictate. That role fell to younger brother John, with whom Tommy had always had a special bond. The task of getting a paraplegic all the way from St Andrews to Whitburn by train must have been an arduous one. Lizzie also came along as best maid, but no other member of the Morris family travelled to West Lothian. Apparently it was that delicate a situation socially.

If further proof was needed that Tommy didn't care what anyone in town thought about the marriage, he provided it by taking the outlandish step of renting for him and his bride an extravagant home. They moved into a large two-storey house in a fashionable neighbourhood then known as Playfair Place, after Sir Hugh Lyon Playfair, saviour of St Andrews. The home had previously been occupied by a family of five and its servant. It rented for the princely sum of £28 a year, the annual salary of most working-class men. In Victorian society it was considered vulgar for a person to flaunt new-found wealth. Old Tom must have cringed at the reaction he knew would be coming from his friends and employers.

As that momentous year drew to a close, Tommy and Margaret learned that their life was about to take an even more dramatic turn. She was pregnant. Their first child would arrive the following autumn.

Eleven

A MORTAL BLOW

————— •◦◉◦• —————

Moving to Playfair Place represented a rite of passage for Tommy. Before marrying Margaret, he may have gained immortal fame and pocketed hundreds of pounds, but like most Scottish men his age, he had never lived anywhere other than his parents' house.

Young Tom wasn't so young any more. He would turn 24 in the spring of 1875. He was head of his own household, awaiting the birth of his first child, perhaps another Tommy to carry on the family name. He and his father had a photograph taken that year, and Tommy looks far different than he did as a teenager. Posed over a shot, his father standing stoically behind him, Tommy sports bushy mutton chops and a thick moustache. He was married now. The fresh-faced style of the young lover no longer suited him. He wanted to look like the grown man he had become.

The house Tommy and Margaret rented was just a short walk from his parents' place at 6 Pilmour Links. It was in a relatively new neighbourhood and featured six spacious rooms. Their baby would be born in a home that offered far more comfort than either of them had known as children. Margaret, especially, must have reflected on how well off her child would be compared to the daughter of a desperately poor miner.

Comfort aside, living at Playfair Place may not have seemed all that different to Tommy. Just as his mother had done back home, Margaret would manage the household affairs. She would choose decor and furnishings, hire a maid to help with cooking and cleaning, and, most of all, prepare for the arrival of their baby come September. Scottish children born in that age needed multiple layers of clothing to ward off the chill. Nearly all of their outfits would be hand-sewn by their mother. Margaret would have had a busy year making clothes for her baby, some to wear during the day, others to sleep in at night. For all of her tasks, she would have sought guidance from *Mrs. Beeton's Book of Household Management*, a weighty tome of advice and recipes that was on every bride's wish list of wedding gifts. Given the skills she'd learned as a maid, Margaret probably needed it far less often than most women.

The harder job for Margaret and Tommy would have been fitting into the social scene in uptight St Andrews. There is no evidence that anyone in town or in the Morris family knew that Margaret had given birth to a child out of wedlock. Not much goes unknown in a small town, however. Even if people didn't know about Margaret's past, it was enough that Tommy had committed the social faux pas of marrying someone from a lower class. He and his bride would not have been warmly received by social barons of the old, grey town.

But what did Tommy care? He had his own friends in the Rose Club. They still met regularly at pubs to discuss events of the day, perhaps Alexander Graham Bell's astonishing success in transmitting sound that year or Matthew Webb's Herculean feat in becoming the first person to swim the English Channel. One club member, a town councillor and poet named George Bruce, wrote this about Margaret. Tommy, he said, 'was united, both in the bonds of affection and wedlock, to a young woman for whom he had the strongest love – and who was in every way worthy of his affection.' Clearly Margaret was welcome in Tommy's circle.

Tommy and Margaret had barely settled into their new home when plans were announced for a foursome that would overshadow all other golf played in 1875. In early September, after the autumn meeting at North Berwick, four titans of the game would face off. It would be Tommy and his father against Willie and Mungo Park, Open Champions all, for £25 a side. At just 36 holes, the foursome would not be a battle on the same scale as a Great Match like Tommy and Davie's marathons in 1873 or the legendary matches between Old Tom and Willie. That did not seem to matter to fans. Whenever the Morrises played against the Parks, reviving that ancient rivalry between St Andrews and Musselburgh, every golfer in the land paid rapt attention.

The timing was awkward for Tommy and Margaret. By 4 September, when the match was to take place, she would have reached the period of her pregnancy known as confinement. In the Victorian era, when delivering babies was far from the routine matter it is today, women spent the final weeks of pregnancy in bed, cared for by family members or midwives as they awaited birth. Tommy must have been aware that Margaret's first child, Helen, had been sickly and died weeks after being born. He also would have known that in the 19th century, giving birth involved substantial risks for both mother and child. Still, Victorian men weren't expected to witness childbirth, and it was hardly uncommon for them to be away from home and miss the delivery altogether. If the timing concerned Tommy, it was not enough to put off the match, which involved a full day's travel by train and ferry to reach North Berwick on the southern shore of the Firth of Forth.

The contest pitting the Morrises and Parks was actually a rematch. In 1874, the golf calendar had been thrown out of whack when the Open was staged in April at Musselburgh, leaving golf fans with no Championship to look forward to come the autumn. North Berwick stepped into the breach by arranging a foursome pitting Tommy and his father against Willie and Mungo for £25 a side. The quaint resort was no stranger to big-money golf. It had been quick to capitalise on the game's surging popularity by staging professional tournaments and high-profile matches to lure vacationers to its beaches and yachtsmen to its harbour.

The match hadn't gone well for the St Andrews men, partly because Old Tom was off form and partly because Tommy's mind was on courting Margaret. The Parks won easily, closing out Tommy and his father on the 16th by going three holes up with two to play. The victory gave Willie and Mungo bragging rights for the next year, and nothing could have pleased them more than rubbing that in. It is unlikely that Willie had forgotten the trouncing Young Tom had given him at Carnoustie in 1867, or that the Park clan had stopped being bitter about the way Willie's match against Old Tom had ended in 1870. Young Tom and his father were proud men too, and were anxious for a chance to redeem themselves, especially Old Tom, who so often took the blame when he and his superstar son went down in a foursome. Years later, historian Everard would write that Tom was seldom 'much better than a drag on his son'.

Throughout the summer, newspapers across Scotland were banging the drums in anticipation of the showdown at North Berwick. Technically, Tommy was no longer Champion Golfer, having lost the last two Opens. But he was still the greatest player the game had ever seen and its biggest attraction. Once he had settled into his new life with Margaret, Tommy resumed his winning ways. In May, he and Old Tom cruised to victory in a foursome against Davie Strath and Jamie Anderson, always a tough tandem. In August at Burntisland, where the ferry departs from Fife, Tommy romped home in a tournament that drew the leading professionals in the game. Davie and Bob Ferguson tied for second, as Old Tom finished fourth. Willie and Mungo plodded in far behind.

The next day, Tommy and his brother Jof took on Ferguson and another Musselburgh pro, Willie Paxton, in a match for 15 shillings put up by the Morris brothers versus five shillings staked on the Musselburgh boys. Tommy didn't play with his younger brother nearly as often as he did with his father. Jof was a solid player, but always a notch below the best golfers of his age and light years behind Tommy. It must have been a fun afternoon for the Morris boys as they won comfortably, going four holes up with just three to play.

By 1 September, when it was time to board the train for North Berwick, Tommy and his father had deservedly emerged as heavy favourites for the big rematch. It must have pained Tommy to leave Margaret behind in St Andrews. She was nearing the end of her pregnancy and their baby could be born any day now. But at least Tommy had the solace of knowing that relatives would be looking after his wife, who by that time would have been confined to her bed at Playfair Place.

The next morning, the action finally got under way at what Horace Hutchinson described as the 'sporting little links of North Berwick', a picturesque nine-hole course criss-crossed by serpentine stone walls. Later expanded to 18 by Davie, the course stretched out along the Firth of Forth. The vantage point features spectacular views across the water to the enormous Bass Rock, with its colony of gannets, and the shores of Fife in the distance.

North Berwick's most dangerous hole was the sixth, known as the Redan. A demanding short hole named after a military fortification, it features a blind tee shot of some 180 yards to a green that is guarded by deep bunkers and slopes wickedly from right to left. Miss above the hole and a three-putt is all but certain. Land in a bunker and any score is possible. The Redan would play a dramatic role in the clash of Open champions and go on to become the world's most imitated par three. Most holes at North Berwick were considered relatively short ones in Tommy's day. But 'little as they are, they are wonderfully full of incident', Hutchinson wrote. 'In fact, the course is practically all hazards, except the putting greens.'

The much-anticipated foursome between the Morrises and Parks was preceded by a tournament for professionals featuring a healthy purse of £20. Gamblers who had risked their fortunes on Tommy and his father had to be second-guessing themselves as they watched the first 18 holes of that event. The St Andrews men seemed to have lost their form. Both Tommy and his father trailed Willie and Mungo after round one, with Old Tom playing especially poorly. The Parks were poised to win the tournament and carry their momentum into the big match. Characteristically, Tommy dug in, finding his game over the last 18 holes and eking out a victory by a single stroke, his second consecutive tournament win.

Moments afterwards, when scorecards were being checked by the referee, a respected lawyer named Hume, all hell broke loose. Bob Cosgrove, a run-of-the-mill professional from Musselburgh, turned in a card that showed his score to be one stroke lower than Tommy's. He loudly demanded that he be given the winner's share of £7. 'Not so fast,' Hume said. He examined Cosgrove's card, along with those turned in by two other Musselburgh men, and ruled that all three of them had been marked incorrectly. That meant every one of those players was disqualified. Young Tom, the referee ruled, had taken first place and the prize money.

The decision opened all the old wounds between upper-crust St Andrews and working-class Musselburgh, antipathy that had boiled for decades as denizens of that struggling town refused to accept what was obvious to everyone else: that St Andrews was and always would be the spiritual home of golf in the kingdom. Willie and Mungo were among those furious about Hume's decision. A foursome pitting Willie and Ferguson against Tommy and Davie was called off. Willie, Mungo and all the top players from Musselburgh stormed off the links, vowing never again to compete against men from St Andrews. The big match was suddenly in jeopardy.

The Park brothers thought better of it with a night to cool off. There was, after all, the tidy sum of £25 at stake, and still fresh in their minds was the satisfying memory of having humbled Tommy and his father the previous autumn. Wouldn't the best revenge for Hume's perceived injustices be to take the haughty St Andrews men down again?

Whatever Willie and Mungo were thinking, at 11 o'clock the next morning the match got under way when Tommy sent a shot sailing off the first tee, the opening salvo in a day of last-minute heroics and unbearable heartbreak. Months of hype in the press brought out an immense crowd, so many people that it was a struggle to contain them even with the use of a gallery rope. 'The prevailing enthusiasm may be guessed from the fact that in the throng the young lady visitors to North Berwick were numerously represented, all of them resolutely sticking to their posts abreast the rope during the four rounds which the foursome comprised,' *The Scotsman* wrote.

It was a crisp autumn morning in North Berwick, marred only by a stiff breeze that blew from the west. The sporting little links was 'rather keen', as *The Scotsman* put it, firm and fast enough to give the greatest golfers in the world all the trouble they wanted. The players made four trips around that nine-hole links, two in the morning and two after lunch. Fans who had awaited this match all summer must have had trouble believing that these four golfers accounted for a dozen Opens between them. Their play was nothing short of embarrassing, a performance *The Scotsman* charitably described as 'middling', 'really unexceptional' and 'not up to form'.

The tone was set on the opening holes. Both teams made six on the first and seven on the second, hardly the stuff of legends. The golf didn't improve as the morning wore on, especially for the Parks. When Willie wasn't spraying a drive, he was topping one into a bunker or leaving a critical putt woefully short. Mungo botched so many shots, especially on the greens, that *The Scotsman's* reporter couldn't hide his contempt. Late in the match, when Mungo finally holed a meaningful putt, the writer grudgingly acknowledged that it 'somewhat redeemed the champion's character'. The Parks fell four holes behind on that first 18 and no doubt headed to the lunch break in a foul mood.

Despite their big lead, Tommy and his father couldn't have been happy with their play either. Old Tom wasn't at his best, but he wasn't as far off form as Tommy. The four-time Open champion missed easy approach shots and failed to conjure up his usual magic on the greens. One could not help but wonder if his thoughts were drifting back to St Andrews. Was Margaret having their baby? Would the child be what every Victorian man wanted, a boy? No one in North Berwick knew it then, but Margaret had gone into labour, and the birth was not proceeding smoothly.

At two o'clock in the afternoon, the players returned for the final two trips around the links. The anxious crowd of Park fans surrounding the first tee had to wonder if their hometown heroes were too far behind at four holes back with just 18 to play.

'By some it might have been thought that the match was over,' noted *The Scotsman*. 'By those more acquainted with the chance of the game, however, the matter was not received with such certainty, and the second start was therefore made with little, if any, abatement in the interest manifested by the onlookers.'

The Parks didn't get the start they needed. They bungled the first hole with an eight to fall five down. But Tommy and his father did not exactly finish them off. They played so feebly on the second that they picked up, and Tommy gave away the fourth with an insanely risky attempt to putt through a bunker. Willie and Mungo responded by frittering away every opportunity the Morrises handed them, including taking three putts at the Redan when two would have won a precious hole. They remained four holes behind as the final nine began. Now the Parks would have to dig deep.

They did just that, playing what *The Scotsman* described as 'a remarkably plucky game'. Willie and Mungo took the first two holes with deft shots around the green as the Morrises found trouble in bunkers and rough. With seven to go, the lead was down to two. The Parks had a realistic chance to rally. They stumbled only once more, losing the fourth, before making their run. Mungo holed that character-saving putt to take the fifth. Willie ratcheted up the tension with another winning shot to the Redan and followed it with a 40-foot putt on seven that rolled in to thunderous applause. Just like that the big match was all square again with two holes left to play.

Now the pressure was squarely on the Morrises, who had led nearly all afternoon. Tommy loved a challenge like that. He had played so miserably all day. Now he had a chance to overcome every one of those misdeeds with a single swing. His shot from the eighth tee was brilliant, sailing far and landing safely. Willie tried to top it with a bomb of his own, but his ball ended up in a hazard from which the Parks couldn't recover. That put the St Andrews men on the brink of victory, one up with one to play.

'The game for the last hole was watched with the greatest of closeness by everyone on the green, the spectators crowding in at times and giving expression to their sympathies in a not very becoming way,' reported *The Scotsman*, taking a swipe at rowdy Park fans. The ninth proved to be a replay of the eighth. Old Tom's tee shot landed in a perfect spot. Mungo's wound up in a tough lie from which the Parks could manage only a half in five. Tommy and his father prevailed by a single hole.

The marquee match of the 1875 golf season may have provided high-pitched excitement on that final nine, but *The Scotsman* could not bring itself to conclude its lengthy report without noting that neither side had played the game spectators expect of champions. 'Last year,' the newspaper noted, 'it may be remembered, a foursome between the same men was gained by the Parks with 3 up and 2 to play. Saturday's game, it should be stated, was not on the whole scarcely so good as that of last season.'

But golf wasn't the reason that afternoon would be remembered forever. No one who was there in North Berwick, and thousands who weren't, would ever forget what *The Scotsman* delicately described as 'a melancholy occurrence' that unfolded on the final green. As Tommy and his father stood triumphant, savouring a victory that restored the lustre they had lost in last year's drubbing by Willie and Mungo, a messenger elbowed his way through the bustling crowd and handed the young superstar a telegram.

Margaret was desperately ill, it said. Tommy and his father must return to St Andrews with 'all possible haste'. One can only imagine the sense of helplessness Tommy must have experienced and the horrifying thoughts that raced through his mind as he read that dire news. In the distance, he could see the north shore of the Firth of Forth, where his wife lay struggling in childbirth, but he and his father both knew it would be all but impossible to get back home at that late hour.

It was after four o'clock when the match ended. By then, there was not another train from North Berwick that could get them back to St Andrews that night. The only choice was to set out by horse-drawn cart, an absurdly difficult journey. Even by train and ferry the trip between towns took six hours. Tommy and his father were just about to take to the road when a wealthy gentleman who spent his summers in North Berwick, J.C.B. Lewis, offered to sail them across the Firth on his yacht.

Father and son readily accepted Lewis's generous offer, although even aboard a yacht they faced a slow and dangerous passage. Sailing from North Berwick to St Andrews – even at top speed in perfect weather – would take well over six hours. The last few hours would be spent sailing in the dark. Even the ferries that crossed the Firth of Forth every day did not sail at night. They closed at sundown.

Lewis's yacht had just made it to the mouth of the harbour, meaning it was still within easy hailing distance, when those who had seen Tommy and his father off were handed a second telegram. Margaret, it said, had given birth to a son. Both mother and child were dead. Everyone agreed there was no sense in calling Tommy and his father back to the dock, 'fearing the shock to the unhappy husband would be too great'.

What passed between Tommy and his father on that long, tense journey will never be known. It would have been nearly midnight, perhaps later, when Lewis's yacht pulled into the pitch-dark harbour at St Andrews and the two of them began the nerve-racking walk through town and up North Street to the home at Playfair Place where Tommy and Margaret had lived for less than a year. Reverend Boyd, the balding shepherd of Holy Trinity, was waiting for them inside the house to break the tragic news. In his memoir, he remembered the scene as one of the most heart-rending he had ever witnessed.

'What can one say in such an hour?' Boyd wrote. 'I will never forget the poor man's stony look; stricken was the word, and how all of a sudden he started up and cried, "It's not true!" I have seen many sorrowful things; but not many like that Saturday night.'

Three days later, on Tuesday 7 September, Reverend Boyd presided as Margaret and her son – can there be any doubt that he, too, would have been christened Tommy? – were laid to rest in the cathedral cemetery at St Andrews. No local newspaper published an obituary of Margaret, wife of one of the town's best-known citizens. The tombstone erected at her gravesite, which would have been ordered by a member of the Morris family, misspelled her maiden name as Drennan, not Drinnen. Those slights are powerful evidence that Tommy's marriage to Margaret was never truly accepted in either St Andrews or the Morris household.

'Young Tom never really recovered from this shock and grief,' Tulloch wrote in his biography. 'He had been married for less than a year, and he was devotedly attached to his wife. Now he had lost her in the saddest, and, to a young husband the most pathetic . . . manner. He went about like one who had received a mortal blow. Even his beloved game failed to rouse him. He lived as if in some trance – all his light-hearted buoyancy gone.'

Twelve

A WINTER OF MOURNING

———————— • ● ◉ ● • ————————

Three days after Tommy's wife and son were laid to rest, the competition that had catapulted him to fame was played again at Prestwick. For the first time since the inception of the Open Championship, there was no one named Morris in the field.

Tommy, his father and his brothers, all in the period Victorians called deep mourning, stayed home at 6 Pilmour Links. Tommy had moved back in with his parents after Margaret's death, no longer comfortable in that large, empty house on Playfair Place. Newspapers took note of Tommy's absence, but with only a veiled reference to the deaths of his wife and son, reflecting journalistic sensibilities of the era. 'Everyone must sympathise with Young Tom Morris, who this year was prevented from entering the list by a severe domestic affliction,' as the *Dundee Courier* put it.

Willie Park, now 42 years old, led a field of 18 players off the first tee on Friday 10 September 1875. He came to the final hole of that Open with a chance to finish in 49 and show the world again why he ranked with the greatest golfers the game had ever seen. Only Tommy had ever scored lower during an Open at Prestwick, with his record of 47 in 1870. It was not to be. Willie sprayed his tee shot on the home hole and settled for a 51, but it was good enough to win his fourth and final Championship.

That Friday afternoon, in the absence of their most feared rivals, the men of Musselburgh savoured the greatest performance they had ever managed in an Open. Defending champion Mungo Park took third and Bob Ferguson came in fourth. Bob Martin, one of Old Tom's favourite employees, salvaged second place for St Andrews, while Davie Strath, still recovering from the shock of his best friend's loss, finished sixth, a dozen strokes off the lead.

Young Tom would not appear again on the links until three weeks after that Open. His friends thought a round of golf might be good for him, take his mind off his suffering, and he was cajoled into playing. On 30 September, during The R&A's autumn meeting, Tommy and Davie paired up with club members and competed in a foursome, just as they had done so often when the young champion was piling up the pounds and becoming the first man to make his living purely from playing golf. Tommy, however, showed little of the bravado and fighting spirit that had characterised his play since his debut a decade ago. Davie and his partner won by five holes.

The next day, Tommy's loyal backers put up the stakes for his first real match since the deaths of Margaret and his son, in hope that the adrenaline of big-money competition would bring back the careworn champion's old fire. He and his father were pitted in a foursome against Davie and Bob Martin, who was in top form after that second-place finish at Prestwick. The skinny, mutton-chopped Martin, at his best, could be as tough as any player in the game who wasn't named Tommy. During the 1870s, Bob won five professional tournaments, among them one of his two victories in the Open Championship.

As always when Tommy and his father were involved, a gallery that seemed to include every golf fan in St Andrews followed the players around the links. At the outset it appeared that the plan to arouse Tommy's competitive spirit had worked. He played brilliantly through the opening holes, dropping putts from everywhere and giving his side a four-up lead with just five holes to play. The match seemed a foregone conclusion. But in that final stretch, Tommy and his father lost their edge. Davie and Bob began winning back holes one by one and had squared the match by the time the foursome reached the 18th tee. There Tommy sealed his team's fate with a badly mishit drive that barely cleared the Swilcan Burn, handing Davie and Bob the hole and the match. Local newspapers and Tulloch's biography concluded that Tommy and his father lost because the champion collapsed emotionally.

'The match seemed to be finished when Tommy broke down in the most complete, though perhaps one cannot add the most unexpected and unaccountable, manner,' the biographer wrote.

Tulloch and the reporters can be forgiven for leaping to that conclusion given the agonies Tommy had endured and how valiantly he had always played when the match was on the line. But they seemed to have forgotten a few key points: that Tommy and his father would never have been in a position to win had Tommy not played such sterling golf for 14 holes; that Davie and Bob ranked with the great golfers of the age and could never be counted out; and most importantly, that Tommy clearly was ready for more golf, because he was back on the links that very afternoon to compete in the annual tournament for professionals at St Andrews.

Tommy joined a dozen leading players for that event, among them Mungo Park and Bob Cosgrove of Musselburgh and former Open champion Tom Kidd. A total of £30 was at stake, with £12 to the winner. Jamie Anderson took the top prize, with

Davie in second and Tommy in fifth. Just six strokes separated the top five. Tommy had suffered an unspeakable tragedy, and obviously was not in peak form, unable to sustain the intensity required to close out a match or a tournament. Still, as he had demonstrated early in the battle against Davie and Bob, he was still capable of brilliant golf, and there was every reason to expect there would be more glories to come.

After everything that had happened since North Berwick, Tommy needed some good news in his life. It came that autumn, as the marriage of his best friend was announced from the pulpit of Holy Trinity. On 21 November 1875, Davie married Agnes Roland, a nurse from Dundee, a city near Carnoustie where Tommy had his breakthrough victory what now seemed ages ago. Tommy surely would have been cheered by the news, but he could not have attended the wedding. In Victorian Scotland, the rituals of mourning were strictly followed. A person whose wife and child had recently died, as Tommy's had, would be expected to return to work, in his case professional golf, but would have been forbidden from attending weddings or other social gatherings.

Four days after Davie's wedding came the announcement that would be the focus of attention in St Andrews for the rest of that long, cold, snowy winter. Tommy's friends continued to think the best prescription for what ailed him was golf, in particular the chance to play in a high-profile match that could add another chapter to his well-established legend. Their opportunity came in the form of a brash challenge issued from south of the border by a famed family of golfers from Westward Ho!, the course Old Tom had laid out on the seashore in North Devon.

Just as Willie Park had done in 1854, when he showed up at St Andrews offering to play any golfer in the kingdom for £100 a side, Arthur Molesworth and his sons came to town with a challenge of their own. The father would back his son Arthur

Jr., a formidable amateur golfer, against any professional for any sum of money as long as he was given strokes. Arthur wanted what was known in those days as a third, or a stroke on six of each 18 holes. This sort of challenge was nothing new for the Molesworths. At both Prestwick and St Andrews, Arthur and his sons – the others were George and Reginald – had taken on leading amateurs in matches, with young Arthur winning easily both times. During his career, Arthur Jr. would also win many club medals at Hoylake.

Tommy's backers were thrilled to accept the Molesworths' challenge. On 25 November 1875, the anniversary of Tommy's wedding, the match against Arthur Molesworth was announced in the press to considerable fanfare. It would be a gruelling affair, 12 rounds over the St Andrews Links in winter. This one match would span as many holes as Tommy and Davie's two historic clashes during the summer of 1873. Thirty-six holes would be played on each of six days, with rest days in between. The stakes were complicated. The sum of £50 rode on the outcome of the match and another £50 on the winner of the most rounds – accounting, of course, for the six strokes Tommy would give Arthur each time. There were also bets on the number of strokes taken by each player over the 216 holes.

While this was an exhibition match – Arthur, after all, was an amateur receiving strokes – it featured all the trappings of a Great Match between professionals. Newspapers from across Scotland and England sent reporters to cover the competition, and untold amounts of money were bet on the various propositions. T.T. Oliphant, an R&A member, was named umpire for the contest. The stakes were held by James Denham, who kept an account of the match that Tulloch reproduced in his biography of Old Tom. The match began on Tuesday 30 November, St Andrew's Day, when Scots commemorate their patron saint.

Even before the first tee shot was struck, it became clear that this battle between Tommy and Arthur would be waged under conditions that would test even the hardiest golfer's mettle. St Andrews is in the northern latitudes. Winters there can be harsh. On the first day of the match, when players arrived for their regular starting time of 10.30 a.m., the temperature hovered near freezing and a cutting wind blew across the links from the north-east carrying flurries of snow. Unfortunately for Tommy and Arthur, the weather would get worse, not better.

Snow fell in St Andrews three times that week. Twice Tommy and Arthur arrived at the first tee to find the links covered in a white blanket, with drifts two feet deep in places. On every hole, they were preceded by men with brooms and shovels doing their best to clear the greens. Both players used balls painted red, so they could be found in that sea of white. They still needed spotters on every fairway, because balls picked up snow as they rolled and became all but invisible again. *The Scotsman*, in its classically understated way, described the conditions as 'unique in the chronicles of golf matches'.

Remarkably, despite the miserable weather, every shot of the match was followed by a multitude of transfixed fans trudging along the snowy fairways. That was either a tribute to Tommy's immense drawing power or a testament to the allure of a spectacle as bizarre as watching golfers slash their way through such ridiculous conditions. Among those following the widespread news reports of the match was a 16-year-old from the Royal North Devon Golf Club named Horace G. Hutchinson. He would go on to become a great golfer and two-time winner of the Amateur Championship, as well as the first English captain of The Royal and Ancient Golf Club of St Andrews.

By the fifth day of the match, conditions were so bad that Tommy sensibly appealed to his backers to put a stop to the madness. Arthur wouldn't hear of it, emboldened by a rare win the previous day. He and Tommy played on. On the final day of the marathon, as the golfers again dodged two-foot drifts and waited for greens to be swept, snow began to fall after the lunch break. Tommy and Arthur played the last 18 holes in the middle of a storm. Shortly after this match, a watercolour was painted of the scene at the High Hole – the 11th at St Andrews – that shows just how absurd it was to play in such weather. It depicts Tommy about to loft a shot over a part of a green still covered with snow. His goal was to land it in a tiny area around the hole that had been cleared for putting. The artist was Major F.P. Hopkins, a famed amateur painter of golfing scenes, as well as a golf writer, who signed his watercolours and writings 'Short Spoon' or 'Major S'.

The match was never close, even though Tommy gave Arthur six strokes every round. Scotland's King of Clubs established an insurmountable early lead – winning the first four rounds and leaving Arthur a dozen holes behind – and never surrendered it. Not surprisingly, given the conditions, the scores Tommy and Arthur turned in often seemed laughable. Tommy took more than 100 strokes in a third of his rounds and broke 90 only four times in a dozen tries. Arthur had nine scores over 100, including one of 125, and came close to breaking 90 only once, when he came in with a 91.

When the competition mercifully ended, Tommy had prevailed on all fronts. He won the match 11 holes up with ten to play. He won three more rounds than Arthur, and he took 1,167 strokes to Molesworth's 1,261. Even if one subtracts the 72 strokes Arthur received during the match, Tommy still finished 22 strokes ahead. He won at least £100 for those who had backed him, a healthy amount of which would have wound up in the champion's pocket. Nevertheless, friends who watched him play could see that the match had taken a lot out of Tommy. A month earlier newspapers reported that he had become 'seriously unwell', although they did not say what ailed him. Playing all those rounds in the cold and snow could not have helped Tommy, physically or spiritually.

'It was evident to all that Tommy was in no condition to play a great match,' Tulloch wrote. 'His play lacked all its old characteristics of spirit and determination. His heart was not in the game. It was, indeed, not very far away – in the snow-clad grave in the old cathedral churchyard, where his wife and baby had been so lately laid. During the progress of the match, he repeatedly said to his friend, Mr Denham, that but for the interest of his friends and backers he would not have continued it.'

The match ended on 7 December, less than three weeks before Tommy would endure the trial that comes to all the newly widowed. He would face the first Christmas without the love of his life and his son, a low point on any journey through grief. 'He continued to be seen on the links and in his old haunts,' Tulloch wrote, 'looking ill and depressed.'

On the Tuesday before Christmas, Tommy took a quick trip to Edinburgh, a favourite haunt of him and his mates from the Rose Club. He needed a change of scenery, and apparently it helped. Tommy came back home on Thursday, three days before the holiday, and was in relatively cheerful spirits considering all he had been through that autumn and winter. He spent Christmas Eve dining quietly with a few friends, likely Davie and other companions from the club, and returned home to 6 Pilmour Links at about 11 o'clock.

His mother Nancy, now 60 years old, had been bedridden with rheumatoid arthritis for years. Tommy was in the habit of spending the last moments of each day talking with her before turning in for the night. He spent Christmas Eve that same way. When Tommy went up to his attic room to go to bed, his father came in to say goodnight, as he always did, and then the young superstar drifted off to sleep.

The next morning, Christmas Day, Tommy didn't come to breakfast at his usual hour and didn't answer when his parents called. A maid was sent to check on him, and she immediately called Old Tom into the room. He found his son dead in bed, looking as if he had never awakened. A trickle of blood was visible around his mouth.

Denham, as a friend of the Morris family, wrote an obituary of the young superstar. In it he said a medical examination determined that Tommy died of an aneurysm in his right lung. A century and a half later, modern physicians would review the evidence and suggest it was likely that Tommy suffered some sort of cardiovascular disaster, probably a ruptured aneurysm of one of the main arteries resulting in fatal bleeding into the right chest cavity. Young Tom Morris was 24 years old.

Tulloch remembered what it was like on that fateful morning in St Andrews: 'The news spread like wildfire over the links and in the city,' he recalled. 'Consternation prevailed everywhere. Christmas greetings were checked on the lips by the question, "Have you heard the news? Young Tom is dead!" or the whispered, "It can't be true, is it, that Tommy was found dead in bed this morning?" Everywhere there was genuine grief for so great a loss – the loss of one who had been the pride of the whole golfing world; everywhere the sympathy with the bereaved father and mother was keen and great. The telegraph conveyed the news to the evening papers, and next morning to some of us among our belated Christmas cards and greetings came this:'

OBITUARY NOTICE

Thomas Morris, jun., died here this morning at ten o'clock.
6 Pilmour Links, St Andrews, Dec. 25, 1875.

Thirteen

FOR GOOD AND ALL

—————————•●◉●•—————————

Christmas Day in the Morris household would
have been spent pursuing the rituals of Victorian
mourning. Every clock in the house would have been
stopped at 10 a.m., the formal hour of Tommy's
death. Every window would have been shuttered, a signal to the
outside world of the tragedy that had befallen the family. Some
families even covered mirrors or turned them towards the wall,
as many Victorians believed mirrors could entrap the spirit of
the dead before it ascended into heaven.

Tommy's body would lie in the parlour until his funeral four
days hence. The night before the burial, family and friends
would gather for dinner, prayers, and the heartbreaking ritual of
wrapping his body in a white linen burial cloth and sealing it in
the coffin. For at least a year afterwards, Old Tom and his sons
would wear black armbands as an outward sign of their sorrow.
The rules were stricter for women. Nancy would dress only in
black for two years. Some Victorian women who lost husbands
or children wore no other colour for the rest of their lives.

Tommy's funeral took place on Wednesday 29 December 1875. Victorian funerals were elaborate and expensive. Many families had to save all their lives to afford to bury their dead. Old Tom spared no expense on the funeral for his famous son. He hired a hearse drawn by black horses adorned with large, black ostrich feathers, as was customary in that era, along with black-clad, top-hatted mourners to lead the procession from 6 Pilmour Links to the cathedral churchyard.

That afternoon, under lowering skies, Tommy's body was carried from the house and placed in the hearse. At precisely 3 p.m., in keeping with tradition, the cortege began its slow, solemn march through St Andrews. Old Tom and Reverend Boyd walked behind the hearse, followed by Tommy's brother Jof, his cousin Jack and his uncle George. Both had travelled from Hoylake for the funeral. Behind them came Davie Strath and Charlie Hunter, an old friend from Prestwick who had followed in Tom's footsteps as keeper of the green there. Nancy stayed home that day, and not simply because she was so ill. In Victorian Scotland, burials were attended only by men. It was not considered proper for women to be at the graveside. Given his infirmities, Tommy's little brother John would have needed help to join the procession. Still, he had made it all the way to West Lothian for his brother's wedding, so it is hard to imagine him missing the funeral. Tommy's sister Lizzie was in America with her husband James and could not have travelled home in time for any of the ceremonies.

Every shop and business in St Andrews closed for the day. No golf was played on the links. Hundreds of men turned out to pay their respects to Tommy, among them golfers from many places in the kingdom where the young superstar had played. Leading citizens of St Andrews were there too. Mourners included Arthur Balfour, who would go on to become prime minister, Robert Chambers of the famed Edinburgh publishing house W & R Chambers, Major Robert Bethune of the Union Club, the town's provost Thomas Milton and its councillors. 'The remains of poor Tommy were yesterday followed to the grave by a large cortege of persons from all quarters, and the town, usually dull at this season, wore its gloomiest as the mournful procession deployed through the streets,' the *St Andrews Citizen* reported.

By the time the hearse reached the churchyard, the procession of sorrowful followers stretched all the way down South Street. What a melancholy sight it must have been, all those black-clad mourners hemmed in on either side by grey stone cottages looking especially dreary under cloudy skies. Among those in the crowd was Andra Kirkaldy, just a teenager then but destined to become the first man hired as professional of The Royal and Ancient Golf Club. He would recall that sad day in his memoir.

'I remember all about it,' he wrote. 'I was 15 years old when death took Tommy away on Christmas Day, 1875. We all felt under a cloud. He was only 24, and his young wife and child died before him. He never got over that blow. It broke his heart.'

Edward Blackwell, who would grow up to be an exceptional golfer and one of the longest drivers of his age, also had powerful memories of that dark day in St Andrews, even though he was only nine years old when Young Tom died.

'I have a picture in my mind of the popular Young Tom, who came to his melancholy end while I was still a child,' he recalled years later in an interview with author Henry Leach. 'He was a favourite with all the youngsters, and one sees him on the links with his Scotch bonnet brimful of the game and proud of his play, and I remember well, young as I was, how I appreciated his slashing, fearless and always attractive style. I remember, too, his sad and sudden death and the gloom it cast over St Andrews, and the farewell tribute that the people paid to their great young golfer at what was in some respects the most imposing funeral that has ever taken place in St Andrews.'

The outpouring of emotion over Tommy's death was deep and

genuine, and in just a few years would lead to a more lasting tribute. There is no denying that he had been something of a 'provocateur', thumbing his nose at convention and living by his own rules. There is no denying that he had been a cocksure, swaggering golfer who flaunted his winnings in ways that didn't always win friends. But there is also no denying that Young Tom was beloved. He had a gift of charisma given to few men.

Not long after his funeral, *Chambers' Edinburgh Journal* published a tribute that recalled Tommy's three victories to win the Belt and reflected reverence for a young man the writer hailed as 'Champion Golfer of the World'. The poem runs for nine stanzas and is written in the romantic, perhaps overwrought style that was fashionable in the Victorian age. It begins:

> Beneath the sod poor Tommy's laid,
> Now bunkered fast for good and all;
> A finer golfer never played
> A further or a surer ball.
>
> Among the monarchs of the green,
> For long he held imperial sway;
> And none the start and end between
> Could match with Tommy on his day!
>
> A triple laurel round his brow,
> The light of triumph in his eye,
> He stands before us even now,
> As in the hour of victory.
>
> Thrice belted knight of peerless skill!
> Again we see him head the fray!
> And memory loves to reckon still
> The feats of Tommy in his day.

In the churchyard, Reverend Boyd, who just three months earlier had presided over the funeral of Tommy's wife and son, said prayers over his coffin before it was lowered into the grave beside Margaret, their baby, and his younger brother Wee Tom.

As his son's body descended to its resting place, Old Tom must have reflected on Tommy's too-brief but remarkable life. How his birth had brightened the darkness that enveloped him and Nancy after the unexpected death of their first born. How Tommy's rise to golfing immortality had brought him fame and money undreamt of when the family lived in cramped quarters in Prestwick, with Tom's club-making shop consuming half the house. How he and Nancy had watched helplessly that dreary winter as Tommy was devastated by the loss of his wife and son. And how his death had moved so many so deeply on this greyest of days in the old, grey town.

Over the years, the story that would be woven into the legend of Young Tom was that he had died of a broken heart. But at that moment in the cathedral churchyard, Old Tom endured a loss so profound that he never gave the slightest credence to that notion. 'If that was true,' he would say many times afterwards, 'I wouldn't be here either.'

Fourteen

ETCHED IN STONE

———————•●●●●•———————

On a late September afternoon, three years after Tommy's death, in the same cathedral churchyard that had been the scene of his family's greatest sorrows, Old Tom experienced one of his life's singular joys.

After The R&A's annual meeting, several hundred of the town's leading citizens gathered at the Morris family gravesite for the dedication of a monument to Young Tom. The *St Andrews Citizen* described it, appropriately, as 'an event which was looked forward to with a degree of mingled feeling'. As the crowd awaited the unveiling, Old Tom and Jof stood proudly in front of them, beside part of the ancient cathedral's stone wall that had been hidden behind a curtain.

Old Tom was 57 years old by then, dressed in his favourite jacket and tie, his beloved pipe put aside on this momentous occasion. His bushy beard was all but white, and he wore it as long as he ever had, a full five inches below his chin. No one understood the 'mingled feeling' of that afternoon better than

Old Tom. He was thrilled, as any father would be, to see his son enshrined in such a place of honour before such a crowd of dignitaries. But even as he savoured that moment, his heart surely must have ached with the memory of so wrenching a loss.

If anyone in that churchyard understood what Old Tom was feeling, it was the son who stood next to him, wearing a Scotch bonnet reminiscent of Tommy's. At 22, Jof was now Tom's eldest son. As he waited for the ceremony to begin, his mind also must have drifted back to that awful Christmas morning when he lost his brother. But Jof's emotions may have been more complicated. He was the one who had grown up following in the footsteps of the superstar, never nearly as good at golf and never nearly as famous or beloved. That had always been evident in Jof's eyes, his stare as wide-eyed and impassive as Tommy's was intense.

The campaign to build Tommy's monument was the work of James Denham, who had raised the first toast on that historic night at Mr Leslie's Inn, when the golfers of St Andrews carried their young champion through the streets in triumphant celebration of a feat for all time. In the weeks after Tommy's death, Denham had circulated a letter to 60 golfing societies in Scotland and England. It read:

'A very general wish having been expressed that a memorial should be erected to the memory of the late Tom Morris Junior, by placing a suitable monument over his last resting place, and as he was widely known and universally admired for his honest and manly exertions by which he rose to the first place in the golfing world, and for his frank and courteous conduct towards all classes, which made him respected wherever golf was played, it has been thought desirable that an opportunity should be afforded to all who knew him and have witnessed his extraordinary golfing powers, of joining in this tribute to his memory.'

All 60 clubs, an honour roll of the 19th century's leading golf societies, subscribed to finance the still-concealed monument before which Old Tom and Jof stood. Much had happened in Old Tom's life since he found his son dead in bed that Christmas morning in 1875, all of it repeating the pattern of elation and despair that had come to define his family's existence.

In March of 1876, three months after Young Tom's death, news came from America that his sister Lizzie had given birth to a son, Old Tom and Nancy's first grandchild. They could not have been more pleased with the name Lizzie and her husband James chose for the child. He was christened Thomas Morris Hunter. Just as Young Tom's birth had done, the baby's arrival lifted the veil of gloom that had descended over the family. The joy, however, did not last through spring. In May, swamp fever swept through Georgia and took the baby two months to the day after his birth.

In September of that same year, Tom received one of the highest honours of his life, a testament to his rising status in the game. That autumn, Prince Leopold, the royal family member who had enjoyed Tommy and Davie's match at Aberdeen, was to become captain of The R&A, an occasion of monumental importance in St Andrews. In keeping with a tradition that continues to this day, His Royal Highness would play his way in as captain by hitting a drive from the first tee. The dashing young prince sported a natty bowler hat for the occasion and played his stroke with a newly made play club presented to him as a gift by Old Tom. Golf's Grand Old Man teed up the incoming captain's ball for the drive, while the corps of caddies waited anxiously down the fairway. The lucky caddie who retrieved the ball and returned it to the prince received a gold sovereign from him, a tradition that has henceforth been followed by all incoming captains of The Royal and Ancient.

It was the following day, after club members had competed for the autumn medals, that Tom received his honour. He was chosen to play as Prince Leopold's partner in a foursome against leading club members Major Lawrence Lockhart and John Whyte-Melville, a beloved former captain who had often played with Tommy. Only a man as respected as Old Tom would be given such an opportunity. He and the prince won handily. Tom would get to shepherd Queen Victoria's youngest son around the links again in 1877, when His Royal Highness welcomed the club's new captain. Those must have been heady days for a man who had started life as the son of a hand-loom weaver and his career as a ball maker's apprentice.

Less than a month after that memorable afternoon, on 1 November 1876, Tom's wife Nancy died. Death, at least, brought her years of suffering from rheumatoid arthritis to a merciful end. Again, Tom and his sons Jof and John were plunged into the rituals of Victorian mourning, the shuttering of the windows, the stopping of the clocks. In less than a year, Old Tom had buried Tommy, Margaret and their son; he had wept over the death of a grandchild in America, and he had borne his wife of 32 years to her resting place in the cathedral churchyard.

His spirits, and those of his two sons, must have risen with the news that in March of 1877, Lizzie would come home from America to fill the void Nancy's death left at 6 Pilmour Links. Their joy was redoubled that June when Lizzie gave birth to a baby girl. She was christened Agnes Bayne Hunter, taking her late grandmother's maiden name. The following May, Lizzie's husband James, one of Tommy's oldest friends, came back to St Andrews to see his daughter. He was among the distinguished guests in the cathedral churchyard waiting to see the unveiling of Tommy's monument.

It was just after 5.30 p.m. on Tuesday 26 September 1878 when the Right Hon. John Inglis, the Lord Justice General of Scotland and the man who had followed Prince Leopold as captain of The R&A, stepped up to say a few words before revealing the monument to Scotland's once and forever King of Clubs. Inglis told the crowd that he would not bother to recite Tommy's golfing achievements, as they were so well known by the cognoscenti of the game assembled before him. 'Every true golfer mourns his loss most sincerely,' the Lord Justice General said in his brief speech, 'for he was not only a prime golfer, but a very fine young man cut off in the prime of his life. But the time of grief has now gone by; and all that remains of Tommy is a pleasant memory.'

With a final nod of thanks to Denham and the man who had helped him lead the fundraising drive and arrange for construction of the monument – Major Robert Bethune, treasurer of the Union Club – Inglis asked that the curtain be pulled back. Carved in relief within an enormous arch made of freestone was sculptor John Rhind's nearly life-sized statue of Young Tom standing over a putt, wearing his jacket and tie and his signature Glengarry bonnet. Beneath the golfer's feet, the Edinburgh artist had carved an inscription written for the occasion by the Very Reverend Principal Tulloch, Vice-Chancellor of the University of St Andrews. It read:

'In memory of "TOMMY", son of Thomas Morris, who died on 25 December 1875, aged 24 years. Deeply regretted by numerous friends and all golfers. He thrice in succession won the Champion's Belt and held it without rivalry, and yet without envy, his many amiable qualities being no less acknowledged than his golfing achievements. This monument has been erected by contributions from sixty golfing societies.'

Years afterwards, in a chapter of his memoir entitled 'Dear Old St Andrews', Andra Kirkaldy would lead readers on a tour of the town, making his first stop the gravesite where Tommy's monument had been unveiled that afternoon. 'Come with me to the cathedral burial grounds,' he wrote, 'and I will show you a strange thing, the like of which is not to be seen anywhere that I know of. There stands the monument to Young Tom Morris, with a carved, lifelike figure of himself in the act of addressing the ball.'

Andra had seen the entire arc of Tommy's life. He was ten when Tommy won the Belt, old enough to be awed but probably too young to be among the crowd carrying him up the links to Mr Leslie's Inn. He was 15 when he watched the young champion's hero's funeral in St Andrews.

During his long life, Andra had witnessed the epochal changes that followed in Tommy's wake. He and every other boy in the caddie yard could see that golf would never be played the same way after Tommy. His fearless style and the daring shots he invented had eclipsed the conservative approach of the game's early stars.

Andra had seen how Tommy's eternal fame sparked an explosion in the popularity of golf, spreading the game 'like Noah's flood'. He had seen golf evolve from a parochial pastime of gentlemen playing afternoon foursomes or battling for club medals to an international spectator sport driven by megastars and championships.

Andra had competed for the fattened purses that transformation made available to professional golfers, who could now harbour dreams of earning enough money to live nearly as well as gentlemen who employed them. He had seen, for instance, Harry Vardon reap an astonishing £4,000 from one of his voyages to America.

And yet he could not get over the idea that the gentlemen of 60 golfing societies would pay to erect a statue in Tommy's honour in the shadow of Scotland's most famous cathedral. 'A memorial in the kirkyard to a golfer!' Andra marvelled.

Even as the monument to Young Tom was unveiled, the Champion's Belt, catalyst of every one of those momentous changes, remained where it had been since that historic afternoon in September 1870, displayed with pride in the Morris household. Over the years, when pilgrims to St Andrews dropped in to chat with the Grand Old Man of Golf, Old Tom loved nothing more than showing off that trophy and recalling the glorious deeds of his famous son. 'Many a time,' wrote biographer Tulloch, 'I have seen the coveted Belt taken out of its case and handled with great reverence by his father.'

In the generations after Tommy, Bernard Darwin, grandson of the famed naturalist and father of all golf writers, would chronicle for *The Times* of London the changes wrought by the rise of the game's first superstar. Darwin lived through the golf boom and walked alongside the prodigies who followed Tommy, documenting the victories that made legends of Harry Vardon, John Henry Taylor, James Braid, Bobby Jones and Ben Hogan. All along, however, Darwin's older friends from St Andrews insisted that there had yet to be born a golfer of Tommy's calibre. It was not as if those men were stuck in the past. They had seen Tommy win six of every ten times he played, a percentage that dwarfs that of every other golfer enshrined among the game's immortals.

Darwin was nothing if not a sentimentalist and hero-worshipper. He wrote that if he could be granted one wish it would be to be transported to Prestwick on the afternoon when Tommy claimed the Belt. 'If by some potent magic one could summon up the past at will,' Darwin mused, 'there is no golfing picture that I should like to see so much as that of Tommy's third win; 149 was his score for three rounds on the 12-hole course, and he finished 12 strokes ahead of the two men who tied for second. Whenever one is too much inclined to laud golfers of the present to the detriment of those of the past, it is always a wholesome thing to remember that score of 149 round Prestwick. There must have been at least one very great golfer in those days.'

FINAL ROUNDS

———————— •●●●● •————————

'A very fine young man cut off in the prime of his life.' Those words from Lord Justice Inglis at the unveiling of Tommy's memorial must have sounded an especially mournful note for his family and fellow competitors. They were left to carry on without the charismatic champion who had been such a transformative force in their lives and in the game that put bread on their tables.

Some would go on to accomplish feats on the links nearly as impressive as Tommy's, although no golfer who had competed in his shadow could generate the same level of excitement as the King of Clubs had during his meteoric career. Others, like Tommy, would die at far too young an age, a sadly common fate in Victorian Scotland.

Only a few, most notably Old Tom, would live long enough to witness how dramatically the game would be changed by the forces Tommy's ascent set in motion. Within a generation, golf would become so popular south of the border that Englishmen would emerge as the dominant players in the Scottish game, an outcome that would have seemed inconceivable when Tommy made his debut at Perth. Even fewer years would pass before English golfers would experience the same trauma they had inflicted on their northern neighbours in 1890 when John Ball became the first man born outside Scotland to win the Open. The new century had barely begun before Walter Travis sailed across the Atlantic from New York to win the Amateur Championship, the first sign of that ever-lengthening shadow British sports writers would come to refer to as the 'American Menace'.

The stories of how life unfolded for Tommy's family, friends and fellow competitors over those formative years for modern golf begin, fittingly, with the tale of the player whose epic matches with the young champion in the summer of 1873 marked a turning point in the game's evolution into a worldwide spectator sport.

DAVIE STRATH

In the waning moments of the first Open after Tommy's death, Davie Strath stood on the tee of the fearsome 17th at St Andrews needing fives on each of the final two holes to win his first Championship. It had been a chaotic afternoon, and it was about to get worse.

The date was 30 September 1876, the day Prince Leopold played his way in as captain of The R&A. With their attention focused on that high honour, the club's officials had overlooked one critically important detail for the Open. They had not reserved tee times for competitors in the Championship. The result was the most disorganised, embarrassing spectacle in the history of the tournament. The 34 golfers competing in the Open had to tee off intermittently with members of the club and other players from St Andrews.

Leading up to the Open, the course had been soaked by heavy rains, making it a tough day for scoring. Davie came in with 86 for the first round, good enough to be tied for a four-stroke lead with Bob Martin. Late in the second and final round, Davie was involved in an incident that left him deeply shaken. On the 14th hole, he pulled his tee shot left and felled a local workman named James Hutton, who was playing on the adjoining fifth fairway. Hutton was fine, despite being hit in the forehead. He got up and walked off the course. Davie, however, was seriously rattled. That mistake and another at 15 cost him precious strokes, but he righted the ship at 16. As he prepared to play the Road Hole, where so many dreams have been dashed, Davie's first victory in the Open seemed within his grasp.

Everything changed when his third shot to the 17th hit a person playing on the green. Having already injured Hutton, Davie must have concluded that his approach shot had absolutely no chance of reaching the hole. He was far too experienced a player to be hitting into the group in front of him on purpose. Davie managed to get his five anyway, but on 18 he faltered just as he had done so often against Tommy. He missed a putt that would have given him the victory. Davie and Bob Martin finished tied at 176.

A play-off ought to have been ordered immediately, but instead the outcome of the Open became mired in controversy. Bob Martin, one of Old Tom's favourite workmen and foursome partners, had many supporters present that day. They filed a protest asking that Davie be disqualified for hitting into the group ahead of him on 17. There was no rule against this, beyond the expectation of courtesy towards other players, and no specific penalty for such an infraction. The R&A Committee met to consider the protest, but it could not come to a decision and postponed its ruling until Monday. Curiously, the committee also ordered that a play-off between Bob and Davie be conducted before the group reconvened.

Davie saw no sense in that. If the decision went against him, there would be no need for a play-off. He refused to do anything before a decision was made. Bob dutifully showed up on Monday morning, walked the course and was declared the winner of the 1876 Open. Davie Strath was not disqualified; he was placed second. Historians through the ages have sided with Davie in the dispute, which left Strath bitterly angry. Bob Martin did eventually get an Open victory without an asterisk, winning the 1885 Championship at St Andrews.

In the years after the debacle of 1876, Davie suffered terribly from tuberculosis, the scourge of the Strath family. A month after Tommy's death, Davie had moved from St Andrews to take a job as golf professional at North Berwick. With Tommy gone, and a wife and two infant children to care for, he needed to be sure where his money was coming from. He played in only one more Open, finishing fourth at a ragged Musselburgh course in 1877. By the following autumn, his tuberculosis had become so severe that Davie decided to take desperate measures.

The latest in medical thinking was that Australia's climate was ideal for those battling tuberculosis. Convinced by his doctors that it was his last, best hope, Davie boarded a ship for Melbourne on 14 October 1878, facing a gruelling three-month journey to the continent Down Under. He fell gravely ill on the final leg of that trip and had to be carried from the ship on a stretcher. He lived just 20 days longer, succumbing to tubercular laryngitis on 28 January 1879. The next day he was buried in an unmarked grave in the Presbyterian section of Melbourne General Cemetery.

It would be 127 years before his grave was rediscovered by Noel Terry, historian for the Royal Melbourne Golf Club. The golf clubs of St Andrews and the Golfing Society of Australia teamed up to raise money for a proper memorial stone at the grave of Tommy's best friend and toughest rival. Sadly, Davie would go down in history as the first to earn faint praise as the greatest player who never won a major championship. The marker was unveiled in a ceremony on 29 January 2006. It reads:

DAVID STRATH
CHAMPION GOLFER
BORN ST ANDREWS, SCOTLAND 1849
DIED MELBOURNE, AUSTRALIA 1879

JAMIE ANDERSON

The first player to raise the level of his game to meet the new standard Tommy had established in golf was, perhaps predictably, the man who had beaten him to setting the record of 77 at St Andrews – Jamie Anderson.

Playing his careful, flawless brand of golf, Jamie won the Open in 1877, 1878 and 1879, repeating Tommy's triple. Jamie's finish in 1878 remains one of the most thrilling in the history of the Championship. He was approaching the ninth tee at Prestwick when he learned that Tommy's younger brother Jof had taken the lead by coming in with his best score ever, a 161. Jamie needed to play the final four holes in 17 strokes – near-perfect golf – to tie with Jof and force a play-off.

'I can dae't wi' a five, a fower, a three and a five,' he told a follower.

Jamie did better than that. He holed his approach shot to the ninth for a three, made his four on the tenth, aced the 11th, matching Tommy's hole-in-one in 1869, and finished with a five on the 12th. It was a fortunate thing that he played those final holes in a remarkable three under fours, because Bob Kirk made a late charge that left him with a long putt on the final hole for a tie. The putt didn't drop, and Bob was so frustrated that he missed the short one coming back. Jamie won by two.

Three years after his winning streak, Jamie's health declined precipitously, an issue complicated by his descent from heavy drinker to hopeless alcoholic. Married with 11 children, he struggled to earn a living as a club and ball maker. He drifted from place to place, first to a small town in Ayrshire, then to Perth, and finally back to St Andrews. There, after a failed business venture, he was declared bankrupt and confined to a poorhouse in Thornton, Fife, where he died drunk and penniless on 16 August 1905. He was 63.

BOB FERGUSON

The steady Bob Ferguson turned out to be the player who came the closest that anyone ever has to matching Tommy's record of four consecutive wins in the Open. Bob ran off three victories in succession after Jamie had done it, winning in 1880 at Musselburgh, in 1881 at Prestwick and in 1882 at St Andrews. His bid to match Tommy ended in a heartbreaking loss at Musselburgh, the course he had grown up next door to and played all his life.

Willie Fernie, a St Andrews native who was then golf professional at Dumfries in southern Scotland, had finished his four rounds at Musselburgh with a score of 159. That was impressive considering that he'd made a disastrous ten on one hole. Bob needed to play brilliantly on the final holes to force a play-off. He did just that, running off a trio of threes to finish in a tie with Fernie. That meant a 36-hole play-off the following day.

Bob came to the last hole of that play-off – a 170-yarder – with a one-stroke lead. Usually imperturbable, Bob stumbled this time. His tee shot missed the green and he could do no better than a four. Fernie's tee shot had landed on the front edge of the green, but it was a long way from the cup. He had two putts to force a second play-off. Miraculously, he holed the first one, a vision that haunted Bob for the rest of his days. Years later, he told an interviewer how he felt watching that putt roll in when he was tantalisingly close to matching the golfer he admired most. 'Absolutely stunned,' he said. 'I dearly wanted to equal Young Tom's record.'

Just as Jamie had done before him, Bob fell ill after his run of Championships. He suffered a bout of typhoid fever and was never the same golfer. He retired to a tranquil life as custodian of the links of Musselburgh, where he taught golf and made and remoulded gutty balls on the side. He died there in 1915 at the age of 67.

BOB KIRK

Two years after Tommy's death, Bob Kirk came back home to St Andrews. He had been away eight years, working as the golf professional at Blackheath, the oldest golf club in England.

Bob had always been a favourite of the Morris family. When he returned to St Andrews, Bob took a job in Old Tom's shop, even though his own father still ran a club- and ball-making operation around the corner.

With Tommy gone, Bob became one of Old Tom's favourite foursome partners. Together they beat some of the game's greats. Like Davie Strath, however, Bob was destined to end his career as one of the greatest players of his time never to win the Open Championship. Twice he had been a distant second to Tommy, with no real chance to win. The last of his three second-place finishes, in 1878 when Jamie Anderson played so miraculously on the final four holes, was the closest he would ever come to claiming the mantle of Champion Golfer.

Never a robust man, Bob's health declined early and he died in 1886 in his home at 4 Pilmour Links, leaving behind a wife and two children. He was 41 years old.

WILLIE PARK

Willie Park, antagonist in the early Open Championships and the tragic finale of golf's favourite father-and-son team at North Berwick in 1875, was 42 years old when Tommy died. He won his fourth Open that year, but it would prove to be his last moment of golfing glory.

All that would remain for Willie was a final battle against his greatest rival. Ever since the fiasco in 1870, when the Great Match between he and Old Tom Morris ended in a bitter dispute, gamblers had been thirsting for a chance to settle accounts between the game's ageing warriors. Their wish was fulfilled in 1882 when Willie clashed with Tom again for £100 a side over the familiar four greens of Musselburgh, St Andrews, Prestwick and North Berwick.

Willie was 48 years old then, Tom nearly 61. Neither played inspired golf, but gigantic crowds turned out to see them nonetheless. Willie surged to an early lead with wins at Musselburgh and St Andrews, sending bettors rushing to his side. Unfortunately for the Honest Toun's favourite son and his backers, Willie's form deserted him at Prestwick, where Tom took a commanding lead that he carried to victory at North Berwick. Willie lost the match when Old Tom went five holes ahead with just three to play on the same course where his young son had been handed that foreboding telegram seven years earlier.

Willie looked frail in the final rounds of that match, even though he was a dozen years younger than his lifelong foe. He would compete in only one more Open, finishing 22nd at his home course of Musselburgh in 1883, the year Willie Fernie crushed Bob Ferguson's hopes with that improbable putt on the final green. By 1894 Willie Park had retired even from club-making, and spent his remaining days watching his son Willie Jr. win two Open Championships and thrive in the golf business.

Old Willie died in his 70th year, on 25 July 1903. Ironically, as he lay on his deathbed, Old Tom was staying in Edinburgh at the home of Mrs Tait having his portrait painted in oils by Sir George Reid, a past president of the Royal Scottish Academy. The portrait had been commissioned a year earlier by The Royal and Ancient Golf Club and has been prominently displayed in the Big Room of the clubhouse since 1903.

Sadly, the death of Willie Park, one of the greatest players the game had ever known, received far less attention from the press than Young Tom's had or Old Tom's would years afterwards. There was no hero's funeral for Willie. His service was private – family only, no friends. In his own lifetime and during the lives of his children, no marker was ever erected in Willie's honour in Musselburgh, the town he had made famous in the annals of golf. That tribute came only recently. Perhaps the reason was that his death came so long after The Honourable Company of Edinburgh Golfers left the Honest Toun for its new home at Muirfield.

One cannot help but wonder what Old Tom thought of how Willie was slighted, given how proud he was of the monument to Tommy, and whether he reflected on how he might be remembered when his time came.

JAMES HUNTER

In the autumn of 1879, James Hunter set sail again for America to tend to his timber business. It had been a year since he stood in the cathedral churchyard to watch the ceremony honouring his childhood friend and brother-in-law. As always, Lizzie stayed in St Andrews with Old Tom and her children. That June, she and James had celebrated the birth of William Bruce Hunter, a brother to young Agnes. Over the next seven years, James would travel back and forth from Scotland to America as he and Lizzie welcomed two more children, Elizabeth Gray and Jamesina, and made dramatic renovations to Tom's workshop and the house at 6 Pilmour Links.

When he came home to St Andrews in 1879, James had assumed the debt of £400 Old Tom had taken on when he bought his house and shop. It could not have happened at a better time, as Tom's finances must have been strained by funeral expenses. Later James gave Tom a loan of £200 to renovate his workshop and convert the room above it into a spacious living quarters for him, Jof and John. It was getting too crowded for all of them in the family home. The new quarters had five rooms, including one that allowed Tom to look out over the green of the 18th hole at St Andrews. Tom took to keeping the Belt in that room with him.

By the end of 1885, when he was once again returning to America, James also had completed extensive renovations to 6 Pilmour Links. The attic room where Young Tom lived and died was replaced with a second storey, and a further addition was made in the back of the house to make room for a modern toilet. The garden was given a makeover too.

The following January, at the age of 37, James Hunter died in Mobile, Alabama in what appeared to be a bizarre drowning. He and two friends had been visiting the captain of a timber ship, toasting into the night. They were clambering by the light of a lantern onto a small boat that would take them back ashore when James fell overboard and never surfaced. An autopsy revealed that he'd suffered heart failure and likely would have died wherever he happened to have been at that moment.

The timber baron's body was returned to St Andrews, and on 19 February 1886, he was buried in the cathedral churchyard next to Tommy's memorial. He left behind a wife, four children and a staggering estate of £12,752. In Scotland during that era, less than 1 per cent of all estates were that large. Lizzie and her children – and by extension Old Tom and his sons – had become extraordinarily rich.

TOM MORRIS AND FAMILY

Tom Morris was 65 years old when James Hunter was laid to rest. He had already outlived his wife, his son-in-law and Tommy, Margaret and their child. He would, in time, survive every member of his family except his grandchildren. His brother George passed away in Hoylake in 1888 after a long illness. His son John, who had struggled all his life as a paraplegic, died of heart trouble in 1893 at the age of 34. Pneumonia took daughter Lizzie in 1898, leaving Agnes to care for Old Tom, Jof and her siblings, William, Elizabeth and Jamesina. In 1906, Jof succumbed to rheumatoid arthritis, just as his mother had done, after years of physical decline and depression.

Amid all this misery, as had been true all his life, Old Tom experienced more than his fair share of happiness. In 1880 he was made an elder of Holy Trinity Kirk, so long a centrepiece of his life. Six years later, the kirk accorded Tom the rare honour of being its representative in Edinburgh at the General Assembly of the Church of Scotland. In 1895, members of The R&A rewarded his years of loyal service by establishing a testimonial fund in his honour, raising £1,240 from members. When invested, together with his salary for life, it paid Tom £150 annually for the rest of his days, three times his starting wage.

Old Tom continued to play professional golf and to lay out and redesign courses into his old age. On his 70th birthday, playing at St Andrews, he went around in a remarkable 73. In 1895, the year he turned 74 and competed in his final Open, Tom played a significant part in building a second course at St Andrews. Forever after the two courses would be known as the New Course and the Old Course. In 1901, Old Tom had the pleasure of seeing his life's work – and especially that of his son Tommy – come to fruition with the formation of the Professional Golfers' Association. He was named the organisation's honorary vice chairman.

By that time, however, there was growing dissatisfaction with the way Tom maintained the links and lorded over golf in St Andrews. Modernisation was the watchword of the age, but Tom still did things the old-fashioned way. It did not sit well with the new men of The Royal and Ancient Golf Club. George Bruce, the town councillor and poet who had been so fond of Young Tom, took to mocking Old Tom in his verse. He branded him the Pope of Golf, not exactly a term of affection in a Presbyterian town.

In 1903, after 40 years as the undisputed authority on golf at St Andrews, Tom was persuaded to resign from his post as keeper of the green. He spent his final years taking walks around the old, grey town and his beloved links, pottering about in his shop, or socialising with friends at the New Club, where he was an honorary member. There he enjoyed afternoons spent in conversation over a pint of blackstrap, a mixture of stout and soda.

On Sunday 24 May 1908, Old Tom made his regular stop at the New Club, although there would be no blackstrap that afternoon. Alcohol was not served on the Sabbath in St Andrews.

He got up to use the lavatory but mistook its door for that of the wine cellar, tumbling down the steep steps, where he was found unconscious. Rushed to St Andrews hospital, he died shortly after arriving of an injury to his skull. He was three weeks from his 87th birthday. Old Tom's funeral surpassed even Tommy's in grandeur, attended by so many that the church did not have room enough for all the mourners. On 27 May 1908, he was laid to rest beneath the memorial to his famous son.

That autumn his surviving grandchildren, led by William Bruce Hunter, sent a letter to The R&A offering to bequeath the Belt to the golf club. 'On behalf of my sisters and myself,' William wrote, 'I beg to ask The Royal and Ancient Golf Club to accept from us the Open Championship Belt, which belonged to our late grandfather, Tom Morris. The Belt was won outright by his son Tommy and he cherished it more than anything in his possession. In offering the Belt to the club, we feel that we are only doing what our late grandfather would have desired.'

The R&A graciously accepted the trophy. It resides now in a glass cabinet in the front hall of the clubhouse, alongside the Amateur Championship trophy and the Claret Jug. The last name inscribed on the silver clasp of that Belt and the first one etched onto the Claret Jug are the same – Tom Morris, Jun.

Postscript

AN AUTHOR'S JOURNEY

———————•●◉●•———————

E very golfer who makes the pilgrimage to St Andrews
experiences a moment of communion with the game's
history. Mine came during a visit to the ancient burial
ground in the cathedral churchyard. There I first laid
eyes on the monument to Young Tom Morris.

Rising to the top of the cathedral's stone wall, nearly twice the
height of an average man, Tommy's memorial stone towers over
every grave in a cemetery where luminaries have been buried for
centuries. Standing before it, with that dashing young man in
the Glengarry bonnet staring down at me, I was as awestruck as
Andra Kirkaldy must have been, given that he made Tommy's
memorial the first stop on his tour of 'Dear Old St Andrews'.

But I could not shake a troubling question. How can golf have
all but forgotten a player who inspired men from nearly every
club that existed in his age, 60 in all, to build such an imposing
monument to his memory? These were wealthy, landed gentlemen.
They were not naturally inclined to honour those born to a lower
class. Tommy's life must have been truly extraordinary.

By the time I left St Andrews, I had become fixated on understanding what Young Tom had done to move men to carve his likeness in stone. I knew that telling his story would be a daunting task. Only a person who understood the full arc of golf history could hope to grasp what Tommy had meant to those men and the game they loved so dearly.

Before making that first trip to St Andrews, I had dabbled in the game's history. Now I would need to earn a Master of Arts in golf. The curriculum would be expansive. It would involve tracing the growth of competitive golf over four centuries, studying the evolution of course design and greenkeeping, learning how the game has been taught and played through the years, and researching the careers of other golfers whose heroics have earned them a place among the immortals.

I began my studies by devouring the Classics of Golf Library, which has lovingly reproduced 69 of the greatest books ever written about the game. The collection includes volumes on every dimension of golf, among them the first biography of Old Tom. The books that comprise the heart of the library, however, are those by Bernard Darwin. His driving ambition seems to have been keeping alive memories of golf's heroes of old as 'the years go ruthlessly on and make dim the brightest of records'. That became my inspiration in telling Young Tom's story.

From the Classics Library, I followed Tommy's trail down other byways. I found memoirs by golfers who had seen him play in his prime. I read histories of seminal clubs like St Andrews and Prestwick. I immersed myself in scholarship about the Morris family and the Victorian era. I pored over biographies of the game's other superstars. I golfed at Prestwick, St Andrews and North Berwick, the scenes of Tommy's greatest feats. I even bought a set of hickory-shafted clubs, though not one as rudimentary as Tommy's, and played with them to understand exactly how hard golf was in his day. Modern players simply have no idea how much easier the game has become.

Equipped with that perspective, I was prepared to scour centuries-old newspaper archives for accounts of Tommy's tournaments and matches. In raw numbers, they told the tale of his march into history. But they were not the treasure trove I had hoped to discover. Reporting in the 19th century, especially early on, was a shadow of the professional enterprise we know today. Writers summarised events, including scant detail, and never interviewed players, not even Tommy. It didn't help that Young Tom and his friends, nearly all educated men, were more inclined to talk in pubs than exchange letters. Even on the most important occasions in his life, records of Tommy's own words are almost non-existent.

Fortunately, insight into the young champion's personality – his dashing, no-holds-barred approach to golf and life – can be found in remembrances by those who knew him or competed against him when he was at the peak of his powers. And, of course, as with all historic figures, Tommy's own actions speak volumes.

The portrait that emerged from all those years of enquiry made it easy to understand why gentlemen from most golf clubs in the kingdom dipped into their own pockets to honour Tommy's memory. They had lived through one of those rare moments in history when genius meets opportunity and nothing is ever the same. They felt duty-bound, as men have through the ages, to make certain the world would never forget.

The reasons Tommy faded from memory became obvious too. For generations, his groundbreaking accomplishments have been obscured by his own harrowing story, the loss of his wife and son in childbirth, and his sad decline and death three months later. If Tommy is remembered at all, it is as the golfer who died of a broken heart.

Tommy has also been hidden in the shadow of his father. Old Tom lived so long and accomplished so much – as a player, as a golf architect, and as a man whose honourable character shaped the game – that he is the only Morris remembered now. More than 100 years after his death, Old Tom's portrait still hangs in golf clubhouses around the world and he is still parodied in television commercials.

If this book has succeeded, Young Tom Morris will be restored to his rightful place in the history of this royal and ancient game. No longer will he be remembered simply as the gifted player who died tragically young or as the precocious son of golf's Grand Old Man.

He will be remembered as a player for all time, a golfer who dominated his generation as only a handful of men have done in 150 years. Every one of those golfers, from Harry Vardon to Tiger Woods, will be talked about as long as fans argue over which player is the greatest who ever lived. Tommy deserves to be part of that conversation.

Most importantly, Young Tom will be remembered as the prodigy who revolutionised the way golf was played, established it as a popular spectator sport and charted the path for its future. He will be remembered as the game's pioneer.

That is what the gentlemen of Britain's 60 golfing societies set out to accomplish all those years ago when they erected a statue of Young Tom on hallowed ground at the Home of Golf in St Andrews.

Stephen Proctor
Wittsend Farm

Appendix

TOMMY'S CAREER

———————— •●◉●• ————————

The record that follows represents a substantial majority of the professional events in which Tommy competed. It does not purport to be comprehensive. Golf coverage was spotty during his era, and there can't be much doubt that he competed in events that went unrecorded or unnoticed. In general, only competitions against other professionals are included. The exceptions are his debut against William Greig and his final Great Match against amateur Arthur Molesworth. Those matches are listed because they contributed so significantly to Tommy's legend. As with any golfer of his era, Tommy would have spent most of his time and earned much of his money by competing as the foursome partner of men from prominent clubs like Prestwick or The R&A.

RECORDS SET

Youngest player ever to win a major championship, aged 17 years, five months and eight days.

Only player ever to win four Open Championships in succession – 1868, 1869, 1870 and 1872 (Championship was not held in 1871).

Took possession of the original Open trophy – the Champion's Belt – with three consecutive victories in 1868, 1869 and 1870.

First player to make a hole-in-one in a major championship, 1869, 8th hole, Prestwick.

Lowest score ever recorded in a 36-hole Open Championship, 149, September 1870.

Set record score for 12-hole course at Prestwick, 47, September 1870.

Tied record for low score at St Andrews, 77, May 1870.

OPEN CHAMPIONSHIP

Tommy entered his first Open Championship at the tender age of 14. During his career, he would play in the Championship nine times.

1865, Prestwick, withdrew. Winner, Andrew Strath, 162.
1866, Prestwick, 9th of 16 on 187. Winner Willie Park, Sr., 169.
1867, Prestwick, 4th of 10 on 175. Winner, Old Tom Morris, 170.
1868, Prestwick, 1st of 12 on 154, by 3 strokes. Second, Old Tom Morris.

1869, Prestwick, 1st of 14 on 157, by 11 strokes. Second, Bob Kirk.

1870, Prestwick, 1st of 18 on 149, by 12 strokes. Second, Bob Kirk.

1872, Prestwick, 1st of 8 on 166, by 3 strokes. Second, David Strath.

1873, St Andrews, T3 of 26 on 183. Winner, Tom Kidd, 179.

1874, Musselburgh, 2nd of 32 on 161. Winner, Mungo Park, 159.

Totals: 9 Championships, 4 wins, 1 second, 1 tie for third. Winning percentage: 44 per cent

STROKE-PLAY TOURNAMENTS

In Tommy's age, there were only two regularly scheduled professional stroke-play competitions – the Open Championship and the St Andrews Professional Tournament. In some years, as noted below, professional tournaments were conducted at both the spring and autumn meetings at St Andrews. In other years, the tournament was held only in the autumn. There was no tournament in years when St Andrews hosted the Open. Tournaments were conducted by other clubs, but not on an annual schedule. What follows is Tommy's record in significant stroke-play tournaments. Given that fields were often small and news reports often incomplete, results are listed simply as wins or losses, except when Tommy withdrew during the competition. News reports frequently do not include the names of all competitors. In cases when Tommy was on the grounds, but not listed as a competitor in the event, it is assumed that he would have played.

1865, St Andrews Professional Tournament, Autumn, LOSS

1866, Perth Open Tournament, LOSS

1866, St Andrews Professional Tournament, Spring, LOSS

1866, St Andrews Professional Tournament, Autumn, LOSS

1867, St Andrews Professional Tournament, Spring, LOSS

1867, Leith Professional Tournament, LOSS

1867, Carnoustie Professional Tournament, WIN

1867, St Andrews Professional Tournament, Autumn, LOSS

1868, Leven Professional Tournament, WIN

1868, St Andrews Professional Tournament, Spring, WIN

1869, St Andrews Professional Tournament, Autumn, LOSS

1869, Burntisland Professional Tournament, WIN

1869, North Berwick Professional Tournament, WIN

1870, St Andrews Professional Tournament, Spring, WIN

1870, St Andrews Professional Tournament, Autumn, WITHDREW

1871, Royal Liverpool Professional Tournament, WIN

1871, St Andrews Professional Tournament, Spring, WIN

1871, St Andrews Professional Tournament, Autumn, WIN

1871, Carnoustie Professional Tournament, LOSS

1872, Musselburgh Professional Tournament, WIN

1872, Royal Liverpool Grand Professional Tournament, WIN

1872, St Andrews Professional Tournament, LOSS

1872, Aberdeen Professional Tournament, WIN

1874, St Andrews Professional Tournament, LOSS

1875, Burntisland Professional Tournament, WIN

1875, North Berwick Professional Tournament, WIN
1875, St Andrews Professional Tournament, LOSS

Totals: 27 tournaments, 14 wins. Winning percentage: 52 per cent

SINGLES MATCHES

Following are the results of Tommy's key singles matches. While some matches consisted of a single round, the majority were contested over 36 holes, which was considered the true test of a champion. A few were Great Matches conducted over multiple days – among them two 108-hole matches against David Strath in 1873 and the 216-hole match against Arthur Molesworth that concluded Tommy's career.

1864 at Perth vs William Greig, WIN
1866 at St Andrews vs David Strath, WIN
1866 at St Andrews vs David Strath, LOSS
1867 at Carnoustie vs Bob Kirk, LOSS
1867 at Carnoustie vs Willie Park Sr., WIN
1867 at Prestwick vs Willie Park Sr., LOSS
1868 at St Andrews vs Bob Ferguson, WIN
1868 at St Andrews vs William Dow, WIN
1868 at St Andrews vs Bob Kirk, LOSS
1869 at St Andrews vs David Strath, WIN
1869 at St Andrews, Musselburgh and Luffness vs Bob Ferguson, WIN
1870 at Westward Ho! vs Bob Kirk, WIN
1870 at Westward Ho! vs Johnny Allan, LOSS
1870 at Prestwick vs Johnny Allan, LOSS
1870 at Musselburgh, North Berwick and Luffness vs Bob

Ferguson, WIN
1871 at Musselburgh vs Bob Ferguson, WIN
1871 at St Andrews vs Bob Ferguson, LOSS
1872 at Musselburgh vs Bob Ferguson, WIN
1872 at St Andrews vs Bob Ferguson, WIN
1873 at St Andrews vs David Strath, LOSS
1873 at St Andrews vs David Strath, WIN
1873 at St Andrews vs David Strath, LOSS
1873 at St Andrews vs David Strath, WIN
1873 at St Andrews vs Bob Ferguson, WIN
1873 at Aberdeen vs David Strath, WIN
1874 at St Andrews vs David Strath, WIN
1874 at North Berwick vs Willie Park, Sr., WIN
1874 at North Berwick vs Willie Park, Sr., WIN
1875 at St Andrews vs Arthur Molesworth, WIN

Totals: 29 matches, 20 wins, 9 losses. Winning percentage: 69
per cent

FOURSOME MATCHES

Following are the results of Tommy's key professional foursome
matches. As with singles matches, most of these contests were
played over 36 or more holes. More than half were played with
his father as a partner, as the pairing was the leading attraction
in golf.

1867, St Andrews, Tommy/William Dow vs Bob Kirk/
Jamie Anderson, WIN
1867, Carnoustie, Young/Old Tom vs Bob Kirk/Bob
Ferguson, WIN
1867, St Andrews, Young/Old Tom vs Andrew Strath/Bob

Kirk, WIN

1868, St Andrews, Young/Old Tom vs Bob Ferguson/David Park, LOSS

1868, Prestwick, Tommy/Johnny Allan vs Willie Park Sr./Bob Kirk, WIN

1869, Musselburgh, Young/Old Tom vs Bob Ferguson/Willie Park Sr., LOSS

1869, St Andrews, Young/Old Tom vs Bob Ferguson/David Park, LOSS

1869, St Andrews, Tommy/David Strath vs Bob Ferguson/David Park, WIN

1869, St Andrews, Tommy/Jamie Anderson vs David Strath/Bob Kirk, LOSS

1869, St Andrews, Tommy/Jamie Anderson vs David Strath/Bob Kirk, WIN

1869, North Berwick, Tommy/David Strath vs Willie Park Sr./Bob Ferguson, LOSS

1869, Prestwick, Tommy/Jamie Anderson vs David Strath/Bob Kirk, WIN

1870, St Andrews, Young/Old Tom vs Jamie Anderson/David Strath, WIN

1871, Royal Liverpool, Tommy/Bob Ferguson vs Bob Kirk/Johnny Allan, WIN

1872, Musselburgh, Tommy/David Strath vs Willie Park Sr./Bob Ferguson, WIN

1872, St Andrews, Young/Old Tom vs David Strath/Tom Kidd, LOSS

1872, Royal Liverpool, Young/Old Tom vs Tom Dunn/Bob Kirk, WIN

1872, St Andrews, Young/Old Tom vs David Strath/David Park, WIN

1873, St Andrews, Tommy/Jamie Anderson vs David Strath/Tom Kidd, WIN

1874, North Berwick, Young/Old Tom vs Willie Park Sr./ Mungo Park, LOSS

1875, St Andrews, Young/Old Tom vs David Strath/Jamie Anderson, WIN

1875, Burntisland, Tommy/Jof Morris vs Bob Ferguson/ Willie Paxton, WIN

1875, North Berwick, Young/Old Tom vs Willie Park Sr./ Mungo Park, WIN

1875, St Andrews, Young/Old Tom vs David Strath/Bob Martin, LOSS

Totals: 24 foursomes, 16 wins, 8 losses. Winning percentage: 67 per cent

CAREER SUMMARY

The lists above show that Tommy competed in at least 89 major events, combining stroke-play tournaments, singles matches and foursomes. He won 54 times for a winning percentage of 60 per cent. Tommy competed in 36 stroke-play tournaments, combining appearances in the Open Championship with other events for professionals. He won 18 times for a winning percentage of 50 per cent. If one eliminates the four losses he piled up as a mere boy, before his breakthrough year in 1867, his winning percentage rises to 56 per cent.

Tommy played David Strath nine times in singles matches, winning six or 67 per cent.

Tommy played Bob Ferguson eight times in singles matches, winning six or 75 per cent.

Tommy played Willie Park Sr. four times in singles matches, winning three or 75 per cent.

CAREER SUMMARY, YEAR BY YEAR

Beginning in 1867, the year Tommy won his first professional stroke-play tournament, the following list shows how he fared annually, as well as his winning percentage for the season. He never won fewer than 45 per cent of his events, and often won 75 per cent or more.

1867
Stroke-play tournaments: Five events, one win
Singles matches: Three events, one win
Foursome matches: Three events, three wins
Total: 11 events, five wins, 45 per cent

1868
Stroke-play tournaments: Three events, three wins
Singles matches: Three events, two wins
Foursome matches: Two events, one win
Total: Eight events, six wins, 75 per cent

1869
Stroke-play tournaments: Four events, three wins
Singles matches: Two events, two wins
Foursome matches: Seven events, three wins
Total: 13 events, eight wins, 61 per cent

1870
Stroke-play tournaments: Three events, two wins

Singles matches: Four events, two wins
Foursome matches: One event, one win
Total: Eight events, five wins, 63 per cent

1871
Stroke-play tournaments: Four events, three wins
Singles matches: Two events, one win
Foursome matches: One event, one win
Total: Seven events, five wins, 71 per cent

1872
Stroke-play tournaments: Five events, four wins
Singles matches: Two events, two wins
Foursome matches: Four events, three wins
Totals: 11 events, nine wins, 82 per cent

1873
Stroke-play tournaments: One event, one loss
Singles matches: Six events, four wins
Foursome matches: One event, one win
Total: Eight events, five wins, 63 per cent

1874
Stroke-play tournaments: Two events, two losses
Singles matches: Three events, three wins
Foursome matches: One event, one loss
Total: Six events, three wins, 50 per cent

1875
Stroke-play tournaments: Three events, two wins
Singles matches: One event, one win
Foursome matches: Three events, two wins
Total: Seven events, five wins, 71 per cent

Notes on chapters

———— •○◉○• ————

One
HERO'S WELCOME

Information on Tommy's arrival at the train station in St Andrews, as well as the celebration that followed at Mr Leslie's Golf Inn, is derived from contemporary reports in the *Dundee Courier* and coverage in the *Fifeshire Journal* by its correspondent Henry B. Farnie.

William Weir Tulloch's quote describing the style of Young Tom Morris comes from that author's biography of the champion's father, *The Life of Tom Morris: With Glimpses of St Andrews and its Golfing Celebrities*. That biography is also the source of background material on James Glover Denham and William Doleman, including Doleman's quote assessing Tommy's place in golf history.

Two

PRESTWICK

Information on Tom and Nancy Morris's early life in St Andrews and Prestwick is derived from a variety of sources, most importantly, *Tom Morris of St Andrews: The Colossus of Golf,* by David Malcolm and Peter E. Crabtree. Other sources include Tulloch's *The Life of Tom Morris,* James E. Shaw's *Prestwick Golf Club: A History and Some Records,* and *Prestwick Golf Club: Birthplace of the Open,* edited by David Cameron Smail.

Information on the introduction of the gutty ball is derived from *A History of Golf,* by Robert Browning; *Great Golfers in the Making,* edited by Henry Leach; *A History of Golf in Britain,* by Bernard Darwin; Badminton Library's *Golf,* edited by Horace G. Hutchinson; Tulloch's *The Life of Tom Morris* and Malcolm and Crabtree's *Tom Morris of St Andrews.* Information on the cost of manufacturing gutty balls is from John M. Olman and Morton W. Olman's *Golf Antiques & Other Treasures of the Game.*

Information on the life and influence of Allan Robertson is derived from Badminton's *Golf,* Leach's *Great Golfers in the Making,* Browning's *A History of Golf* and Tulloch's *The Life of Tom Morris,* as well as contemporary newspaper reports.

Horace Hutchinson's quote about the pre-eminence of the St Andrews Links is from his essay 'Some Celebrated Links' in Badminton Library's *Golf.*

Information about the difficulties of life in the Victorian age and the quote from A.A. Milne about living with hunger are drawn from Ruth Goodman's *How to be a Victorian: A Dawn-to-Dusk Guide to Victorian Life.*

Both Old Tom Morris's description of his earliest days in golf and his statements about the events leading up to his argument with Allan Robertson over the gutty ball are from Leach's *Great Golfers in the Making.*

The location of Tom Morris's first golf shop was discovered in 2015 in the archives of the University of St Andrews by historian Roger McStravick and reported on the website www. cybergolf.com.

Allan Robertson's quote about how the gutty ball would not fly as well as the feathery – and the details of the scene in which he purposely tops a ball teed up by his caddie – are from Tulloch's *The Life of Tom Morris*.

Three
THRUST AND PARRY

Information about the predominance of match play in golf's early history is drawn from Browning's *A History of Golf*, H.S.C. Everard's *History of The Royal and Ancient Golf Club of St Andrews* and Tulloch's *The Life of Tom Morris*, among other sources. Everard's history is the source of his quote about the preference for match play.

Information on clubs keeping bet books is drawn from *Challenges and Champions: The Royal and Ancient Golf Club, 1754–1883*, by John Behrend and Peter N. Lewis.

In addition to H. Thomas Peter's *Reminiscences of Golf and Golfers*, information about The Great Foursome of 1849 is drawn from Browning's *A History of Golf*, Badminton Library's *Golf*, Tulloch's *The Life of Tom Morris* as well as contemporary newspaper reports. The description of umpire Sir David Baird as 'magnificent and pompous' is from *Challenges and Champions*, by Behrend and Lewis.

Allan Robertson's statement about Willie Park – 'He frichtens us a' wi' his lang driving' – is from Tulloch's *A Life of Tom Morris*.

Information about the near death of golf in the early 19th century is drawn from Malcolm and Crabtree's *Tom Morris of St Andrews*.

Information about the institution of the Open Championship

is drawn from Browning's *A History of Golf*, Shaw's *Prestwick Golf Club: A History and Some Records* and David Stirk's essay 'The Belt', which appears in Smail's *Prestwick Golf Club: Birthplace of the Open.*

Four
MASTER MORRIS

Information about the debut of Tom Morris Jr. at the Perth Open Tournament of 1864 is drawn from Peter Baxter's *Golf in Perth and Perthshire*, as well as contemporary newspaper reports preserved in *The Scrapbook of Old Tom Morris*, edited by David Joy. The direct quote from Willie Park – 'For why have ye brought your laddie, Tom,' as well as Tom Morris's reply – are drawn from Malcolm and Crabtree's *Tom Morris of St Andrews.*

Information about the history of the professional tournament at St Andrews is from *Lewis's Professional Golf 1819–1885*, along with contemporary newspaper reports.

Information about the Battle of the Clans is drawn from an online article by historian Robert Gunn entitled 'Clan Battle of 1396'.

Information about Tom Morris's return to St Andrews is drawn from Badminton's *Golf*, Everard's *History of the Royal & Ancient Golf Club*, Tulloch's *Life of Tom Morris*, Malcolm and Crabtree's *Tom Morris of St Andrews* and newspaper reports preserved in *The Scrapbook of Old Tom Morris.*

Information about the possibility that Young Tom Morris went to work in Glasgow is based on Baxter's *Golf in Perth and Perthshire* and original research revealed by Malcolm and Crabtree in *Tom Morris of St Andrews.*

Descriptions of Young Tom Morris's competitors in St Andrews in the mid-1860s are drawn from Everard's essay 'Some

Celebrated Golfers' in Badminton Library's *Golf.*

Information about Victorian dress and grooming is from Goodman's *How to be a Victorian.*

Information about Old Tom Morris's purchase of his home and shop is drawn from Malcolm and Crabtree's *Tom Morris of St Andrews.*

Details of Young Tom Morris's breakthrough victory at Carnoustie in 1867 are drawn from reports in the *Dundee Courier* and other sources.

Five
THE GIFT OF GOLF

Bob Ferguson's memories of Young Tom Morris and his invincible putting are drawn from George M. Colville's *Five Open Champions and the Musselburgh Golf Story.*

Reverend W. Proudfoot's description of Tommy as 'the embodiment of masterful energy', as well as Willie Park's quote about Tommy swinging 'clean off his feet' are from John Kerr's *The Golf Book of East Lothian.*

Descriptions of Tommy's play and putting are drawn from Badminton's *Golf,* Leach's *Great Golfers in the Making,* Browning's *A History of Golf,* Tulloch's *The Life of Tom Morris* and Malcolm and Crabtree's *Tom Morris of St Andrews.*

Tommy's quote about his father's inability to hole short putts is from Tulloch's *The Life of Tom Morris.*

The story about the letter sent by James Wolfe Murray to the 'Misser of Short Putts, Prestwick' is from Badminton's *Golf.*

Andra Kirkaldy's statements about Tommy are from his memoir *Fifty Years of Golf: My Memories.*

Details about the difficulties of putting on early greens are from Willie Park Jr.'s *The Art of Putting.*

Details of Tommy's golf in 1868 – including the Open Championship and the autumn tournament at St Andrews – are from newspaper reports in the *Fife Herald, Glasgow Herald,* clippings preserved in *The Scrapbook of Old Tom Morris,* David Stirk's essay 'The Belt' and the British Golf Museum.

Details of A.H. Doleman's first reference to par and what would constitute perfect golf on Prestwick's 12-hole course are drawn from the United States Golf Association's online article 'History of Handicapping'.

Six
DASHING NEW BREED

Information about the relationship between gentlemen golfers and professionals is drawn from Horace G. Hutchinson's essay 'Professionals and Caddies' in Badminton's *Golf,* among other sources.

The stories of how caddies behaved are from Andra Kirkaldy's memoir *Fifty Years of Golf: My Memories.*

Information about Young Tom's terms for playing with gentlemen in foursomes was drawn from Malcolm and Crabtree in *Tom Morris of St Andrews,* as well as an interview with co-author Crabtree.

The story of Young Tom and R.J.B. Tait sharing a hotel room is from Tait's essay 'Random Reminiscences' in *The Golf Book of East Lothian.*

The story of Walter Hagen at Deal is from *The Walter Hagen Story, by The Haig Himself.*

Information about Scottish incomes in the 19th century is drawn from a scholarly article by W.W. Knox entitled 'A History of the Scottish People: Poverty, Income and Wealth in Scotland 1840–1940'.

Details of the formation of The Rose Golf Club of St Andrews are drawn from contemporary reports in the *St Andrews Citizen*, Malcolm and Crabtree's *Tom Morris of St Andrews*, the interview with Crabtree, and notes Malcolm wrote for the University of St Andrews Library about a collage created by photographer Thomas Rodger and displayed at the Rose Club Ball.

Information about the Chartist movement, in particular statistics on the number of new voters, is drawn from *The English & Their History*, by Robert Toombs, as well as other sources.

Information about the 1869 golf season and the Open Championship is drawn from contemporary reports in the *Fife Herald* and *Ayr Advertiser*, newspaper clippings preserved in *The Scrapbook of Old Tom Morris* and the British Golf Museum.

Seven

1870

Details of the match between Old Tom Morris and Willie Park are drawn from the *Fife Herald*, the *Dundee Courier*, and contemporary newspaper clippings preserved by Morris family friend James Glover Denham that is recounted in Tulloch's *The Life of Tom Morris*, among other sources.

Tommy's statement 'The hole'll no come to you: be up!' is from J. Gordon McPherson's *Golf and Golfers Past and Present*.

Details of Young Tom's record-tying round of 77 at St Andrews are from the *Dundee Courier*, as well as clippings preserved in *The Scrapbook of Old Tom Morris*.

Details of Tommy's winning of the Champion's Belt are drawn from the *Fifeshire Journal*, *The Scrapbook of Old Tom Morris*, Tulloch's *The Life of Tom Morris* and Malcolm and Crabtree's *Tom Morris of St Andrews*.

Charles B. Macdonald's comparison of Young Tom and Bobby Jones is from his book, *Scotland's Gift: Golf*.

Eight
TOMMY TRANSCENDENT

Details on the growth of professional golf during Tommy's lifetime and afterwards are from Lewis's *Professional Golf 1819– 1885*. The same paper is the source of information about the growth of golf clubs, along with an article from *History Today* magazine by John Lowerson entitled 'Scottish Croquet: The English Golf Boom, 1880–1914'.

The quote from Old Tom Morris – 'I could cope wi' Allan myself, but never wi' Tommy' – is from H.S.C. Everard's essay 'Some Celebrated Golfers' in Badminton Library's *Golf*.

Details on the history of the university match between Oxford and Cambridge and its impact are from Robert Browning's *A History of Golf*.

Information about the career of Leslie Balfour-Melville is drawn from an online article by the British Broadcasting Corporation written by Roy Murray. Balfour-Melville's quote, 'I can't imagine anyone playing better than Tommy did,' is from Bernard Darwin's *A History of Golf in Britain*.

The story of Peter Brodie backing Young Tom at North Berwick is from The Golf Book of East Lothian.

Details of summertime pursuits in St Andrews in 1871 are from a variety of sources, including Badminton's *Golf*, George Colville's *Five Open Champions and the Musselburgh Golf Story*, Tulloch's *The Life of Tom Morris* and Malcolm and Crabtree's *Tom Morris of St Andrews*.

Details of Prestwick's offer to extend the Open Championship to St Andrews and Musselburgh are from James E. Shaw's *Prestwick Golf Club, A History and Some Records*, H.S.C. Everard's *History of The Royal and Ancient Golf Club from 1754 to 1900*, and Behrend and Lewis's *Challenges and Champions*.

Nine
DREAM SEASON

Details on the Rose Club Ball are drawn from reports in the *St Andrews Citizen*, Malcolm's notes to the photographic collection of the University of St Andrews Library and Malcolm and Crabtree's *Tom Morris of St Andrews*.

Details of the golf tournaments and challenge matches staged in 1872 – at Musselburgh, Hoylake, St Andrews and Aberdeen – are drawn from the *Fife Herald*, the *Aberdeen Journal*, the *Dundee Courier* and *The Field* magazine.

Bernard Darwin's description of the links at Hoylake is from his book, *The Golf Courses of the British Isles*.

Bob Ferguson's recollection about him and Willie defeating Tommy and Davie in a match at North Berwick is drawn from Colville's *Five Open Champions and the Musselburgh Golf Story*.

Ten
MATCH PLAY

Details about the life of Tommy's wife, Margaret, in particular her shaming before the elders of the parish church in Whitburn, are based on groundbreaking research by Malcolm and Crabtree first published in their *Tom Morris of St Andrews*.

Details of the golf matches in 1873 between Young Tom Morris and Davie Strath are drawn from accounts in *The Scotsman*, *The Field*, clippings preserved in *The Scrapbook of Old Tom Morris*, Badminton Library's *Golf*, Tulloch's *The Life of Tom Morris* and *Tom Morris of St Andrews*. Davie Strath's lament about not putting as well as Tommy is from *The Golf Book of East Lothian*.

Information about Victorian courtship is from avictorian.com, an online source devoted to life in that era.

Details of the party Old Tom held on the day of his son's wedding are from an article preserved in *The Scrapbook of Old Tom Morris*.

Eleven
A MORTAL BLOW

The quote from George Bruce about Tommy's marriage is from his book *Destiny: And Other Poems*.

Details of the foursome in 1875 at North Berwick featuring the Morrises and the Parks are drawn from reports in *The Scotsman* and the *St Andrews Citizen*.

Horace Hutchinson's description of North Berwick golf course is from his essay 'Some Celebrated Links' in Badminton Library's *Golf*.

Details of the night time sail across the Firth of Forth from North Berwick are drawn from multiple sources, among them reports in *The Scotsman*, A.K.H. Boyd's *Twenty-Five Years of St Andrews*, Tulloch's *The Life of Tom Morris* and *Tom Morris of St Andrews*.

The quote from the Rev. A.K.H Boyd describing Tommy's reaction to the death of his wife and son is from his book *Twenty-Five Years of St Andrews*.

Twelve
A WINTER OF MOURNING

Details of Tommy's return to golf after his wife's death are drawn from Tulloch's *The Life of Tom Morris* and *The Scrapbook of Old Tom Morris*.

Details of Tommy's marathon match with Arthur Molesworth are from a variety of sources, including the *Dundee Courier*, the

St Andrews Citizen, the *Western Times*, *The Scrapbooks of Old Tom Morris* and records kept by James Glover Denham that were reprinted in Tulloch's *The Life of Tom Morris*.

Thirteen
FOR GOOD AND ALL

Information about Victorian mourning rituals is from avictorian. com, a website devoted to life in that era.

Details of Tommy's funeral in St Andrews are drawn from reports in the *St Andrews Citizen* as well as Tulloch's *The Life of Tom Morris* and Malcolm and Crabtree's *Tom Morris of St Andrews*.

Andra Kirkaldy's statements about Tommy's funeral are from his memoir *Fifty Years of Golf: My Memories*.

Edward Blackwell's memories of Tommy and his funeral are from an interview he gave to Henry Leach for that author's book *Great Golfers in the Making*.

Old Tom's response to the notion that his son died of a broken heart is drawn from Tulloch's *The Life of Tom Morris*.

Fourteen
ETCHED IN STONE

Details of the ceremony in which the monument to Young Tom was unveiled – including the quotes from the Rt Hon. John Inglis – are from a newspaper clipping preserved in *The Scrapbook of Old Tom Morris*.

James Denham's letter asking for subscriptions to pay for Tommy's monument is quoted from Tulloch's *The Life of Tom Morris*.

Andra Kirkaldy's reflections on the life of Young Tom are from his memoir *Fifty Years of Golf: My Memories*.

Details of the births and deaths in the Morris family during the years between Tommy's death and the unveiling of his monument are from Malcolm and Crabtree's *Tom Morris of St Andrews* and Tulloch's *The Life of Tom Morris*.

Bernard Darwin's musings about wishing he had seen Tommy win the Belt are from his book *The Golf Courses of the British Isles*.

Fifteen
FINAL ROUNDS

Details of the 1876 Open Championship and the controversial decision regarding Davie Strath are drawn from multiple sources, among them Browning's *A History of Golf*, Badminton Library's *Golf*, Tulloch's *The Life of Tom Morris* and Malcolm and Crabtree's *Tom Morris of St Andrews*.

Details on the discovery of Davie Strath's gravesite are from an online article by Mike Clayton, published on golfobserver.com, as well as *Tom Morris of St Andrews*.

Details on Jamie Anderson's family life are from Roger McStravick's *St Andrews: In the Footsteps of Old Tom Morris*.

Details of the last match between Old Tom and Willie Park are from Tulloch's *The Life of Tom Morris*.

Information about developments in the Morris family in the years after Tommy's death are drawn from multiple sources, principally *Tom Morris of St Andrews*.

The letter written by the Morris grandchildren to The Royal and Ancient Golf Club on the occasion when they presented the Belt to the club as a gift from their late grandfather is quoted from *Tom Morris of St Andrews*.

Bibliography

———•●◉●•———

NEWSPAPERS/MAGAZINES

Aberdeen Journal
Ayr Advertiser
Dundee Advertiser
Dundee Courier
Fife Herald
Fifeshire Journal
Glasgow Herald
Haddingtonshire Courier
St Andrews Citizen
The Field
The Scotsman
Western Times

ARTICLES

Clayton, Mike, 'Finding Davie', Golfobserver.com (2006).

Gunn, Robert, 'Clan Battle of 1396', Scottish History Online (1890).

Knox, W.W., 'A History of the Scottish People: Poverty, Income and Wealth in Scotland, 1840–1940', Scottish Cultural Resources Access Network (1997).

Lewis, Peter N., 'Professional Golf 1819–1885', British Golf Museum, Paper for De Montfort University (1998).

Lowerson, John, 'Scottish Croquet: The English Golf Boom, 1880–1914', *History Today*, Vol. 33, No. 5 (1983).

Malcolm, David, 'Notes on the St Andrews Rose Golf Club', University of St Andrews Library Photographic Archive (2010).

Murray, Roy, 'A Sporting Nation: Leslie M. Balfour-Melville,' British Broadcasting Corporation (2014).

No author cited, 'Famous British Golf Courses: Prestwick', *The American Golfer*, Vol. 1, No. 4 (1909), pp. 209–220.

No author cited, 'Famous British Golf Courses: St Andrews', *The American Golfer*, Vol. 1, No. 2 (1908), pp. 79–91.

No author cited, 'Notes: Young Tom Morris Gets 20 Days Older', Associated Press (2006).

No author cited, 'Victorian Days: the Courtship Ritual', Visit a Victorian.com (No date cited).

No author cited, 'Victorian History: Victorian Funerals and Mourning', Visit a Victorian.com (No date cited).

BOOKS: GENERAL

Balfour, James, *Reminiscences of Golf on St Andrews Links* (Edinburgh, 1887).

Baxter, Peter, *Golf in Perth and Perthshire: Traditional, Historical and Modern* (Perth, 1899).

Behrend, John and Lewis, Peter N., *Challenges and Champions: The Royal and Ancient Golf Club 1754–1883* (St Andrews, 1998).

Boyd, A.K.H., *Twenty-Five Years of St Andrews* (London, 1892).

Browning, Robert, *A History of Golf* (London, 1955).

Bruce, George, *Destiny: And Other Poems* (St Andrews, 1876).

Clark, Robert, *Golf: A Royal and Ancient Game, Extracts from the Original 1875 Edition* (Midlothian, 1984)

Colville, George M., *Five Open Champions and the Musselburgh Golf Story* (Musselburgh, 1980).

Darwin, Bernard, *Golf Between Two Wars* (London, 1944).

Darwin, Bernard, ed., *A History of Golf in Britain* (London, 1952).

Darwin, Bernard, *James Braid* (London, 1952).

Dodson, James, *The American Triumvirate: Sam Snead, Byron Nelson, Ben Hogan and the Modern Age of Golf* (New York, 2012).

Everard, Harry Stirling Crawford, *History of The Royal and Ancient Golf Club from 1754–1900* (Edinburgh, 1907).

Frost, Mark, *The Greatest Game Ever Played* (New York, 2002).

Frost, Mark, *The Grand Slam: Bobby Jones, America and the Story of Golf* (New York, 2004).

Geddes, Olive M., *A Swing Through Time: Golf in Scotland, 1457–1744* (Edinburgh, 2007).

Goodman, Ruth, *How To Be A Victorian* (London, 2013).

Hagen, Walter, with Margaret Seaton, *The Walter Hagen Story: by The Haig Himself* (New York, 1956).

Haultain, Arnold, *The Mystery of Golf* (New York, 1908).

Hilton, Harold H., *My Golfing Reminiscences* (London, 1907).

Hutchinson, Horace G., *The Book of Golf and Golfers* (London, 1899).

Hutchinson, Horace G., ed., *The Badminton Library: Golf* (London, 1890).

Hutchinson, Horace G., *Fifty Years of Golf* (London, 1914).

Jones, Robert T. Jr. and Keeler, O.B., *Down the Fairway* (New York, 1927).

Jones, Robert T. Jr., *Golf Is My Game* (New York, 1960).

Joy, David, compiled by, *The Scrapbook of Old Tom Morris* (Chelsea, MI, 2001).

Keeler, O.B., *The Bobby Jones Story: The Authorized Biography* (Chicago, 2003).

Kerr, John, *The Golf Book of East Lothian* (Edinburgh, 1896).

Kirkaldy, Andra, *Fifty Years of Golf: My Memories* (New York, 1921).

Kirsch, George B., *Golf in America* (Chicago, 2009).

Labbance, Bob, *The Old Man: The Biography of Walter J. Travis* (Chelsea, MI, 2000).

Labbance, Bob, *The Vardon Invasion* (Ann Arbor, MI, 2008).

Leach, Henry, ed., *Great Golfers in the Making* (London, 1907).

Lee, James P., *Golf in America* (New York, 1895).

Lema, Tony, with Gwilym S. Brown, *Golfer's Gold: An Inside View of the Pro Tour* (Boston, 1964).

Lewis, Peter N., *The Dawn of Professional Golf: The Genesis of the European Tour 1894–1914* (New Ridley, 1995).

Low, J.L., *F.G. Tait: A Record* (London, 1900).

Macdonald, Charles Blair, *Scotland's Gift: Golf* (New York, 1928).

Macdonald, Robert S. and Wind, Herbert Warren, *The Great Women Golfers* (Stamford, CT, 1994).

Malcolm, David and Crabtree, Peter E., *Tom Morris of St Andrews: The Colossus of Golf 1821–1908* (Royal Deeside, 2008).

McPherson, J. Gordon, *Golf and Golfers Past and Present* (Edinburgh, 1891).

McStravick, Roger, *St Andrews in the Footsteps of Old Tom Morris* (St Andrews, 2014).

Nicklaus, Jack, with Herbert Warren Wind, *The Greatest Game of All: My Life in Golf* (New York, 1969).

Oliver, Neil, *A History of Scotland* (London, 2009).

Olman, John M. and Olman, Morton W., *Olmans' Guide to Golf Antiques and*

Other Treasures of the Game (Cincinnati, 1991)

Peper, George, *The Story of Golf* (New York, 1999).

Peter, H. Thomas, *Reminiscences of Golf and Golfers* (Edinburgh, 1890).

Robb, George, *Historical Gossip about Golf and Golfers* (Edinburgh, 1863).

Sagebiel, Neil, *The Longest Shot: Jack Fleck, Ben Hogan and Pro Golf's Greatest Upset at the 1955 US Open* (New York, 2012).

Sampson, Curt, *Hogan* (Nashville, 1996).

Sampson, Curt, *The Slam: Bobby Jones and the Price of Glory* (Emmaus, PA, 2005).

Sarazen, Gene, with Herbert Warren Wind, *Thirty Years of Championship Golf* (New York, 1950).

Shaw, James E., *Prestwick Golf Club: A History and Some Records* (Glasgow, 1938).

Smail, David Cameron, ed., *Prestwick Golf Club: Birthplace of the Open, the Club, the Members and the Championships, 1851 to 1989* (Prestwick, 1989).

Sommers, Robert, *The US Open: Golf's Ultimate Challenge* (New York, 1987).

Stephen, Walter, *Willie Park Jr.: The Man Who Took Golf to the World* (Edinburgh, 2005).

Stirk, David, *Golf: The Great Club Makers* (London, 1991).

Tombs, Robert, *The English & Their History* (London, 2014).

Tulloch, William W., *The Life of Tom Morris: With Glimpses of St Andrews and its Golfing Celebrities* (London, 1908).

Wade, Don, ed., *The US Open: One Week in June* (New York, 2010).

Wind, Herbert Warren, *The Story of American Golf: Its Champions and Its Championships* (New York, 1975).

BOOKS: GOLF ARCHITECTURE

Darwin, Bernard, *The Golf Courses of the British Isles* (London, 1910).
Doak, Tom, *The Confidential Guide to Golf Courses* (Chelsea, MI, 1996).

Hunter, Robert, *The Links* (New York, 1926).

Klein, Bradley S., *Discovering Donald Ross* (Chelsea, MI, 2001).

MacKenzie, Dr. Alister, *Golf Architecture: Economy in Course Construction and Greenkeeping* (London, 1920).

Shackelford, Geoff, *Masters of the Links: Essays on the Art of Golf and Course Design* (Chelsea, MI, 1997).

Simpson, T. and Wethered, H.N., *The Architectural Side of Golf* (Stamford, CT, 2005).

Thomas, George C. Jr., *Golf Architecture in America: Its Strategy and Construction* (Los Angeles, 1927).

BOOKS: GOLF INSTRUCTION

Armour, Tommy, *How to Play Your Best Golf All The Time* (New York, 1953).

Aultman, Dick and Bowden, Ken, *The Methods of Golf's Masters: How They Played and What You Can Learn From Them* (New York, 1975).

Boomer, Percy, *On Learning Golf* (London, 1942).

Hilton, Harold, *Modern Golf* (New York, 1913).

Hutchinson, Horace G., *Hints on the Game of Golf* (Edinburgh, 1886).

Jones, Ernest, with Innis Brown, *Swinging into Golf* (New York, 1941).

Jones, Robert T. Jr., *The Basic Golf Swing* (Garden City, NY, 1969).

Miller, Johnny, *Breaking 90 with Johnny Miller* (New York, 2000).

Nelson, Byron, with Larry Dennis, *Shape Your Swing the Modern Way* (New York, 1976).

Park, William, Jr., *The Game of Golf* (London, 1896).

Park, William, Jr., *The Art of Putting* (Edinburgh, 1920).

Penick, Harvey, with Bud Shrake, *Harvey Penick's Little Red Book: Lessons and Teaching from a Lifetime in Golf* (New York, 1992).

Simpson, Walter G., Sir, *The Art of Golf* (Edinburgh, 1887).

Travis, Walter J., *Practical Golf* (New York, 1901).

Vardon, Harry, *The Complete Golfer* (New York, 1905).

Vardon, Harry, *The Gist of Golf* (New York, 1922).

Vardon, Harry, compiled and edited by Herbert Warren Wind and Robert S. Macdonald, *Vardon on Golf* (Stamford, CT, 2002).

Venturi, Ken, with Al Barkow, *The Venturi Analysis: Learning Better Golf from the Champions* (New York, 1981).

Wethered, H.N., *The Perfect Golfer* (London, 1931).

Wethered, Joyce, *Golfing Memories and Methods* (London, 1934).

Woods, Tiger, *How I Play Golf* (New York, 2001).

BOOKS: GOLF LITERATURE

Bingham, Joan and Owen, David, *The Lure of the Links* (New York, 1997).

Campbell, Patrick, *How to Become a Scratch Golfer* (London, 1963).

Darwin, Bernard, *Out of the Rough* (London, 1932).

Darwin, Bernard, *Playing the Like* (London, 1934).

Darwin, Bernard, *Golf* (London, 1934).

Darwin, Bernard, *Golfing By-Paths* (London, 1946).

Darwin, Bernard, edited by Peter Ryde, *Mostly Golf* (London, 1976).

Darwin, Bernard, with editors Robert S. Macdonald and Ian R. Macdonald, *The Happy Golfer: A Collection of Articles from The American Golfer Magazine, 1922–1936* (Stamford, CT, 1997).

Feinstein, John, *The Majors: In Pursuit of Golf's Holy Grail* (Boston, 1999).

Jenkins, Dan, *The Dogged Victims of Inexorable Fate* (Boston, 1970).

Jenkins, Dan, *At the Majors: Sixty Years of the World's Best Golf Writing from Hogan to Tiger* (New York, 2009).

Keeler, O.B., *The Autobiography of an Average Golfer* (New York, 1925).

Laney, Al, *Following the Leaders: A Reminiscence by Al Laney* (Stamford, CT, 1991).

Leach, Henry, *The Spirit of the Links* (London, 1907).

McKinlay, S.L., *Scottish Golf and Golfers: A Collection of Weekly Columns from the Glasgow Herald, 1956–1980* (Stamford, CT, 1992).

Nash, George C., *Letters to the Secretary of a Golf Club* (London, 1935).

Plimpton, George, *The Bogey Man* (New York, 1967).

Price, Charles, ed., *The American Golfer* (New York, 1964).

Rice, Grantland, with Claire Briggs, *The Duffer's Handbook of Golf* (New York, 1916).

Shaw, Joseph T., *Out of the Rough* (London, 1940).

Silverman, Jeff, ed., *Bernard Darwin on Golf* (Guilford, CT, 2003).

Ward-Thomas, Pat, *The Lay of the Land* (Stamford, CT, 1990).

Wind, Herbert Warren, *On Tour with Harry Sprague* (New York, 1958).

Wind, Herbert Warren, *Herbert Warren Wind's Golf Book* (New York, 1973).

Wind, Herbert Warren, *The Complete Golfer* (Stamford, CT, 1991).

Wind, Herbert Warren, *An Introduction to the Literature of Golf* (Stamford, CT, 1996).

Wodehouse, P.G., *Divots,* originally published in Britain as *The Heart of a Goof* (New York, 1923).

Wodehouse, P.G., *Golf Without Tears*, originally published in Britain as *The Clicking of Cuthbert* (New York, 1919).

Historical chronology and synopsis

———•⦿◉⦿•———

1457: The first known reference to golf is made in an edict by King James II, a Scotsman. He bans football and golf as 'unprofitable sports' that distract men from practising the archery needed to defend the realm. This suggests golf was popular in Scotland for at least a generation before that date. The ban is largely ignored.

1612: The first known reference to a feathery golf ball is made in a will in Edinburgh. The feathery remains the ball of choice for more than 200 years. Complicated to manufacture – it is made by stuffing hen, duck or goose feathers into a leather casing – the ball creates a class of workman who will, some two centuries later, become the first professional players.

1724: The first known report about a game of golf appears in the press in Edinburgh. It involves a match for 20 guineas a side between Alexander Elphinstone, son of Lord Balmerino, and Captain John Porteus of the Edinburgh City Guard. Elphinstone wins.

1744: The first known golf competition occurs when the city of Edinburgh, responding to a petition from gentlemen golfers, provides a silver club to be competed for annually on the Links of Leith. The direct result of this gift is the formation of The Honourable Company of Edinburgh Golfers. The club later moves to Musselburgh and, eventually, to Muirfield.

1754: The Society of St Andrews Golfers is formed. In 1834, it will become The Royal and Ancient Golf Club of St Andrews.

1766: Blackheath Golf Club is formed near London, becoming the first golf club in England.

1815: Allan Robertson, a famed feather ball maker and the first player to be hailed as Scotland's Champion Golfer, is born in St Andrews.

1819: The first known reference is made to a professional golf tournament, a competition for caddies and club and ball makers, held at St Andrews as a complement to the autumn meeting of the Society of St Andrews Golfers. The stakes are put up by society members. Over time it evolves into the only tournament other than the Open Championship to be conducted annually during the early years of competitive golf.

1821: Tom Morris, the father of Young Tom, is born in St Andrews on 16 June.

1833: Willie Park, the great golfing rival of the Morrises, is born in Musselburgh.

1834: King William IV bestows his royal patronage on The Society of St Andrews Golfers. The club is renamed 'The Royal and Ancient Golf Club of St Andrews'.

c.1836–37: Tom Morris is apprenticed to Allan Robertson as a golf ball maker. He remains Robertson's apprentice until 1848.

1842: Jamie Anderson, who would become one of Young Tom's toughest opponents, is born in St Andrews. He is the son of popular local figure and ball maker David 'Old Daw' Anderson.

1843: The St Andrews Mechanics' Golf Club is formed, an organisation for local businessmen but later also respectable artisans and caddies.

1844: Tom Morris and Agnes (Nancy) Bayne are married.

1845: Bob Kirk, also the son of a local ball maker, is born in St Andrews. He too will be among Young Tom's friends and competitors on the links.

1846: Tom and Nancy Morris celebrate the birth of their first child, a son named Tommy, affectionately known as Wee Tom.

A new ball made from gutta-percha, the sap of trees that grow in

Malaysia, begins circulating around St Andrews and Edinburgh. Within a few years the gutty ball makes the feathery obsolete and revolutionises the game of golf.

1848: Tom Morris leaves his apprenticeship in a dispute with Allan over the gutty and opens his own shop, making clubs and balls.

1849: David Strath, of a well-known golfing family, is born in St Andrews. He will become Young Tom's best friend and greatest rival. Together they will help transform the Scottish game into a sport popular in England and eventually around the globe.

Tom Morris and Allan Robertson defeat Willie and Jamie Dunn in The Great Foursome of 1849, a match over three courses for the extravagant sum of £400. It will be remembered as the greatest golf competition in the early history of the game.

1850: Wee Tom Morris, Tom and Nancy's first son, dies on 17 April in St Andrews. He is buried in what becomes the family plot in the cathedral churchyard.

1851: Tom and Nancy celebrate the birth of a second son, also named Tommy. Young Tom, born on 20 April, will become the greatest golfer of his age and one of the game's immortals.

In June, Tom accepts the position of keeper of the green at Prestwick Golf Club in Ayrshire. The family moves from St Andrews to western Scotland, and Tom lays out the classic 12-hole links of Prestwick.

1852: A daughter, Elizabeth, is born to Tom and Nancy on 20 January at Prestwick.

1856: A third son is born to Tom and Nancy on 8 January. He is christened James Ogilvy Fairlie Morris, after Tom's patron, the man who was instrumental in his going to Prestwick as keeper of the green. The newborn son would later in life be affectionately known as 'Jof'.

c.1856–63: Young Tom begins his education. He enrols first at the Burgh School of Prestwick but later moves to the prestigious Ayr Academy, one of the leading educational establishments in Scotland. He studies alongside the sons of wealthy merchants and landed gentlemen, an experience that makes him different from every professional golfer of his age.

1857: The first nationwide golf competition – The Grand National

Tournament – is held at St Andrews. It is a foursome competition between gentlemen players from prominent clubs. Blackheath Golf Club wins and to celebrate, publishes an extravagant lithograph which was sent to each club that took part.

1859: Allan Robertson dies of jaundice in St Andrews. He was 44 years old.

Tommy's youngest brother, John, is born in Prestwick on 25 September, with a hip deformity that prevents him all of his life from walking.

1860: On 17 October, Prestwick introduces the first nationwide competition for professional golfers, the tournament that becomes the Open Championship. Willie Park wins, with Tom Morris second. The prize is a Challenge Belt made of red Moroccan leather with an ornate silver buckle. The rules state that any player who wins three consecutive times receives the Champion's Belt as his personal property.

1861: Tom Morris wins the second Open Championship, conducted as usual during the autumn meeting of the Prestwick Golf Club.

1862: Tom wins the third Open Championship by a record 13 strokes, putting him in a position to claim the Belt as his own the following autumn.

1863: Willie Park denies Tom the Belt by winning the fourth Open Championship.

1864: Young Tom, at the age of 12, makes his golfing debut in April at Perth. His match against a local star of the same age, William Greig, draws a larger crowd than the one that watched his father win the Perth Open the previous day by 14 strokes.

In October, Old Tom wins his third Open Championship. It is the first time a winner is awarded a prize other than the Belt. Tom receives £6.

In December, Tom moves his family back to St Andrews, having resigned from Prestwick in August after receiving an offer to become keeper of the green for The Royal and Ancient Golf Club.

1865: Young Tom makes his Open Championship debut at the age of 14. He withdraws before the final round. Andrew Strath, Davie's elder brother, wins the Championship.

1866: Young Tom finishes ninth in his second Open Championship. Willie Park wins for the third time.

1867: Young Tom wins his first professional tournament, defeating an extraordinarily tough field of 32 competitors over the links of Carnoustie. He is 16 years old.

Young Tom finishes fourth in the Open. His father wins his fourth and final Championship.

Even then it wasn't until 1867, when Tommy was a teenager, that a putting green was built for women and the St Andrews Ladies Golf Club was formed, the first in the world.

1868: Young Tom wins his first Open Championship, with a record score of 154 for 36 holes. He becomes, aged 17, the youngest player to win what is now called a 'major', a record that stands to this day. His father finishes second.

In February, Tommy and Davie Strath are instrumental in forming The Rose Golf Club of St Andrews, a club for the more educated young men in town. The club's members would play an important role in spreading the Scottish game around the globe.

1869: Young Tom wins his second Open Championship, with a score of 157, putting him in a position to claim the Belt the following autumn.

Liverpool Golf Club, destined to be the most influential club in England, is formed at Hoylake, a small fishing village on The Wirral.

1870: Tommy wins his third consecutive Open Championship, making the Belt his personal property. He is 19. His score for the first of three 12-hole rounds is an astonishing 47, a new record for Prestwick. His final score of 149, also a record, will not be equalled as long as the Open is played over 36 holes. The change to 72 holes does not come until 1892.

In April, Tom and Willie Park play a Great Match over three courses. It is their fourth high-stakes clash. Willie had won two of the previous three. It ends in a bitter dispute over crowd control and the result is voided. Massive press coverage of this competition, Tommy's quest for the Belt and other high-stakes matches marks the beginning of golf's evolution into a popular spectator sport.

In May, Tommy matches the scoring record of 77 for St Andrews set by Jamie Anderson. Tommy's score attracts more attention as it is made in the play-off of a professional tournament.

Buoyed by his status as Scotland's undisputed Champion Golfer, Young Tom begins around this time to set his own terms for competing in foursomes with gentlemen, who had always controlled what players earned. This represents a historic first step on the road to equality for professional golfers, viewed then as second-class citizens.

On 5 December, Colonel James Ogilvy Fairlie dies. Old Tom's mentor and friend was 61 years old.

1871: No Open Championship is held for the first time in a decade, as The Royal and Ancient and The Honourable Company debate a proposal by Prestwick to purchase a new Open trophy and rotate the event among the nation's three leading clubs, the beginnings of the modern Championship rota.

1872: St Andrews and Musselburgh agree to the proposal from Prestwick. A new trophy, the Claret Jug, is purchased and the Open resumes. Tommy wins again, becoming the only player with four consecutive victories, a record that stands to this day. New rules state that the Claret Jug cannot become any player's personal property. Instead winners are awarded a gold medal.

In April, Tommy wins the first major golf tournament in England, The Grand National Tournament at Royal Liverpool. The club puts up an unheard of purse of £55, with £15 to the winner, and pays the travel expenses of all the competitors. This represents a turning point in the history of the professional game.

1873: Tommy and Davie Strath play two Great Matches at St Andrews, with each winning one. Conducted in July and August, the matches generate extravagant wagering and extraordinary press coverage. More than any single event, Tommy and Davie's matches cement golf's future as a popular spectator sport throughout Great Britain and the world. They are also remembered as the finest display of golf seen up to that time.

Young Tom begins courting Margaret Drinnen, a coal miner's daughter from West Lothian who is employed as a housemaid to a wealthy couple in St Andrews.

Tom Kidd, a local caddie, wins the first Open conducted at St Andrews, dethroning Tommy as Champion Golfer. Tommy ties for third in a record field of 26.

1874: Tommy marries Margaret in Whitburn on 25 November. His parents do not attend. Tommy and his bride move into a spacious home in St Andrews. Margaret discovers she is pregnant.

In April, Mungo Park, Willie's younger brother, wins the first Open held at Musselburgh, which hosts the Championship six months earlier than usual as part of The Honourable Company's spring meeting. Tommy finishes second in another record field of 32.

1875: In early September, as Tommy and his father are defeating Willie and Mungo in a match of Open champions at North Berwick, they receive news that Margaret is struggling in childbirth. Tommy and his father rush home from the event via yacht only to learn the tragic news that both Margaret and the child, a son, are dead.

Three days after Tommy's wife and son are laid to rest, the Open is played at Prestwick. For the first time in its history, no one named Morris is in the field. Tommy, his father and his brother Jof remain at home in deep mourning. Willie Park wins his fourth and final Championship.

In late November and early December, Tommy plays a marathon match of 216 holes against amateur Arthur Molesworth, of the famed family of golfers from Westward Ho! The match is conducted in bitter winter weather, including a final round played in a snowstorm. Tommy wins easily despite giving Arthur six strokes in every round.

On Christmas morning, Young Tom's father finds his son dead in bed, with a trickle of blood coming from his mouth. Doctors would later determine that an artery to his heart had burst, killing him instantly. Tommy was 24 years old.

Four days afterwards, Young Tom is buried in the cathedral churchyard, next to his wife, son and younger brother, in the most elaborate funeral seen in St Andrews to that time. Every business in St Andrews closes and no golf is played on the links.

1876: Nancy Morris dies of chronic rheumatoid arthritis in St Andrews on 1 November. She was 52 years old.

The first Open after Tommy's death is conducted at St Andrews, on the same day Prince Leopold plays his way in as captain of The Royal and Ancient. Bob Martin and Davie Strath finish in a tie. No play-off occurs, but Martin is awarded the victory following a controversial dispute over whether Strath should be disqualified for hitting into a group playing in front of him on the 17th green. Jof Morris finishes third, his best result ever.

1878: A striking memorial to Young Tom, financed by 60 leading golf clubs in Scotland and England, is unveiled in the cathedral churchyard at

St Andrews. It dwarfs every tombstone in that ancient cemetery.

1879: Davie Strath dies of tuberculosis in Australia, having travelled there in a desperate attempt to improve his health.

1885: The first Amateur Championship is inaugurated at Royal Liverpool. Allan Macfie wins. The following year a trophy is created for the event featuring an effigy of Tom Morris on its top.

1887: Jof Morris equals the record of 77 at St Andrews set by Young Tom and Jamie Anderson. His father makes a trade card to celebrate his two sons having accomplished that feat.

1893: In April, Tom's son John dies in St Andrews after suffering a heart attack. He was 34 years old.

1894: Work begins on an additional course at St Andrews, to be named the New Course. It opens the following year. Thereafter the original links is known as the Old Course.

1895: By now firmly established as the Grand Old Man of Golf, Old Tom plays in his final Open Championship at St Andrews.

1898: In June, Tom's daughter Lizzie dies of pneumonia in St Andrews. She was 46 years old.

1901: The first rubber-cored ball, known as the Haskell, makes its appearance in tournament golf as Walter Travis uses it to win the US Amateur Championship. The following year Sandy Herd uses the Haskell to win the Open, and the gutty is doomed. The Haskell, named after its inventor, Coburn Haskell, flies so much farther than the gutty that it changes the game forever, launching the unceasing quest for distance that dominates golf to this day.

1902: The Professional Golfers' Association is formed. Old Tom is named honorary vice-captain.

1903: Old Tom resigns as keeper of the green at St Andrews. Eight years earlier, The Royal and Ancient had raised a fund for him that, together with his salary for life, paid him £150 annually for the rest of his days.

Tom's great rival Willie Park dies in Musselburgh. His funeral is private, family only. Willie was 70 years old. Until recently, no memorial was ever erected to him in the town he made famous in the annals of the game.

1905: Jamie Anderson, who had won three consecutive Opens beginning in 1877, dies penniless in a poorhouse in Fife, having fallen ill and descended into alcoholism. He was 63 years old.

1906: In April, Old Tom's son Jof dies in St Andrews after years of suffering with rheumatoid arthritis. He was 50 years old.

1908: On 24 May, Old Tom Morris dies in St Andrews from a head injury suffered when he falls down a flight of stairs at the New Club, where he was an honorary member. His funeral surpasses even Young Tom's in grandeur, attracting so many mourners that the church can't contain them all. Tom Morris was 86 years old.

That autumn, the grandchildren of Tom Morris donate his prized possession – the Belt won by his son Tommy – to The Royal and Ancient Golf Club. It resides today in a cabinet inside the clubhouse, beside the Amateur Championship trophy and the Claret Jug.

1915: Bob Ferguson, Tommy's great rival from Musselburgh, dies. He was 67 years old. Bob, too, won three consecutive Opens after Tommy's death, beginning in 1880. He nearly tied Tommy's record of four consecutive victories, losing to Willie Fernie in a heartbreaking play-off in 1883.

Acknowledgements

No person who undertakes a book about the Morris family could do so without acknowledging a debt of gratitude to David Malcolm and Peter E. Crabtree, the authors of *Tom Morris of St Andrews: The Colossus of Golf, 1821–1908*. Their book is without peer as an exhaustive study of the man, his family, and his era. It blazes the trail that all other historians must follow. Given the focus of this book, it is particularly important to note that nearly everything that is known about Margaret Drinnen, the unlikely woman who became Young Tom Morris's wife, is the result of groundbreaking research done by those two historians.

I am especially indebted to Peter Crabtree. He has been extraordinarily generous in offering his advice and taking the time to painstakingly review my manuscript. His attention sharpened the story immeasurably. Peter was also kind enough to grant me permission to use photographs from his private collection in this book. I owe him more than I will ever be able to repay. Sadly, Dr Malcolm passed away in 2011.

Others who kindly granted permission to use photographs for this book include Lady Sylvia Morrow, historian and collector Archie Baird, The Royal and Ancient Golf Club of St Andrews, the University of St Andrews Library, and Sheila Walker, the great-great-granddaughter of Old Tom Morris.

I am also grateful to Peter N. Lewis, a distinguished historian for The Royal and Ancient and former director of the British Golf Museum. He was kind enough to speak with me while I was doing research for this book in St Andrews and to share with me some of his revelatory work on the early history of professional golf.

More than anything else, writing this book has reinforced my lifelong belief that librarians and their institutions are precious assets to any community. Oliver Kay, one of my favourite golf partners and a gifted librarian, spent untold hours tracking down rare volumes I desperately needed and scouring Scotland's newspaper archives for reports of Tommy's exploits. I could never have written this book without his help.

The Cupar Library in Scotland also provided critical assistance by providing me with hard-to-find articles from its extensive collection of local newspapers, among them the *St Andrews Citizen* and the *Fifeshire Journal*. I could not have been more impressed with the patient assistance they provided to an unknown American author. It is proof, if any is needed, of the dedication of librarians the world over.

Writing a book also requires the support of family and friends. Every member of my family – my wife, Mara, my son, Bob, and my daughter, Cori – buoyed my spirits throughout this project and served as a sounding board for my ideas. Nothing I have ever achieved in life could have been accomplished without them, especially not without my wife of 35 years. Few people have Mara's gift for critical analysis, and no one could be a better partner in life.

Gladys Ramirez, a former newspaper colleague, graciously agreed to design early manuscripts for me, complete with mock covers and interior photographs. Her work not only inspired me as a writer, but also proved helpful to the many friends who took the time to read the manuscript and offer thoughtful comments that greatly improved the book. These include Mike Waller, Frank Vega, Larry Moore, Mac Liebert, Christian Roettgers, Daniel Danichek, and Lee Horwich.

Michael and Rosalie Pakenham, two dear friends and gifted journalists, served as my first editors for this project. Their encouragement throughout the process and their insightful suggestions improved the result in more ways than I could enumerate. Sadly, Michael passed away in 2018.

Doug Swanson, another fellow journalist and acclaimed author, also took time from his busy schedule to read the manuscript and provide precisely what I had expected from him, penetrating analysis that was essential to elevating the quality of the storytelling.

Mason Champion, my first golf coach, had the wisdom to assign readings along with his practice drills. Among them was George Peper's book, *The Story of Golf*. In many ways, that is where this journey began. I will always be grateful to Mason for insisting that his students become acquainted with the history of the royal and ancient game.

I owe a special debt of gratitude to the Horschel family – my friends Bill and Kathy, their son Billy, a top-ranked professional golfer, and his wife, Brittany. In 2015, when Billy competed in the Open Championship at St Andrews, the Horschels invited me along, gave me a free room in their flat, and treated me as a member of their family. That trip was essential to researching this book. I will never be able to thank them enough for that invitation, as well as others they have extended over the years.

Two friends from Florida, Terry Mulreany and Randy Hennis,

also provided moral support that helped keep me on task during the long process of writing and rewriting.

Finally, I want to thank my brother and sister-in-law, Scott and Marijo McLachlan. They own Wittsend Farm, where this book was written. Nearly a decade ago now, Scott and Marijo invited me and Mara to buy a home attached to their farm and make Wittsend a family compound that we share with them and their two children, Patrick and Elizabeth. That has done more for me as a writer than they will ever understand. I have been blessed to spend afternoons reflecting on the morning's work while looking out over gorgeous acres of white picket fences and horses. Wittsend has provided the kind of quiet, contemplative environment in which any writer could thrive.

A note on the writing

This book is a narrative history. Its ambition is to tell the story of Young Tom Morris in a way that engages readers without straying from the documented record of his life. That record is limited, presenting a challenge in telling the story the way a narrative ordinarily unfolds, scene by scene. I have studiously avoided the temptation to create scenes, describing only those that could be reconstructed based on news reports or memoirs written by a person who lived in Tommy's age and saw him play. The same is true of quotes attributed to characters in this book. All of them were recorded by a contemporary of the person speaking. The one liberty I have taken is the historian's prerogative to interpret the meaning of events based on my extensive research, and to state my case with the voice of authority. Finally, as all of the events in this story take place in Scotland and England, I have elected to use grammar and spelling as it is practised in the birthplace of the game.

Index

C

caddies, role of 19, 59, 60, 79, 91, 102, 113, 205
Campbell, James 15
Cardinal Bunker, Prestwick 81
Cardinal's Nob, Prestwick 79
Carnoustie Golf Club 43, 62, 93, 112, 126, 209
Challenge matches 87
Chambers, Robert Jr 74, 75, 145
Chambers' Edinburgh Journal 147
Champion's Belt 1-3, 29, 30, 56, 62, 79, 83, 84, 87, 88, 147, 153-55, 166, 169, 208, 215
Chartist Movement 64
Clans, Battle of (Perth, 1396) 33
claret jug (Open trophy) 104, 169, 211, 215
cleek, use of 47, 48, 91, 92, 103
Coltness Iron Company 110
Colville, George 66
Conacher, James 94
Cosgrove, Bob 128, 137
Crichton, James 35
crowd trouble 73, 74, 113, 132

D

Daily News 112
Dalrymple, John H., 10th Earl of Stair 83
Darwin, Bernard 26, 82, 98, 155, 171
Deal Golf Course 62, 82
Denham, James Glover 2, 4, 38, 139, 141, 142, 150, 153
Dickens, Charles 13
Disraeli, Benjamin 52
Doleman, Alexander 54, 80, 81
Doleman, William 4, 51, 54, 55, 105
Dow, William 33, 52
Drinnen, Margaret – see Morris, Margaret
Drinnen, Walter and Helen 110
Dudgeon, Robert 74
Duncan, George 52

Dundee Advertiser 76
Dundee Courier 75, 135
Dunn, Jamie 23-26, 206
Dunn, Willie 23-27, 206
Dye, Peter 54

E

Eglinton, 14th Earl of 29, 30
Eglinton Medal 12
Elphinstone, Alexander 204
Everard, H.S.C. 18, 39, 40, 86, 93, 107, 117, 126

F

Fairlie, Col James Ogilvy 9, 22, 28, 29, 31, 72, 78, 83, 92, 95, 104, 210
Farnie, Henry Brougham 3, 79, 84, 89, 92, 95
feather golf balls (featheries) 14, 15, 47, 204, 205
Ferguson, Bob 38-40, 43, 45, 52, 56, 72, 75, 77, 91, 92, 96, 97, 101, 114, 116, 117, 120, 127, 137, 162, 163, 165, 215
Fernie, Willie 162, 163, 165
Field, The 102, 105, 106, 115
Fife Herald 52, 57, 68
Fifeshire Journal 3, 28, 63, 76, 79, 92
food shortages 11
Foreman's (pub) 74

G

Golf
   as a game for everyone 16
   as a gentlemen-only sport 20, 87
   as a global game 88, 154
   as a spectator sport 4, 154, 211
   at a low ebb 27
   balls 13-16, 47, 50, 80, 82, 204-06, 214
   betting on 18, 21-23, 33, 66, 72, 88, 113, 115, 164, 211
   caddies 19, 59, 60, 79, 91, 102, 113
   foursomes 17, 18, 23-26

T

U

V

W